ASSUMING NAMES

A CON ARTIST'S MASQUERADE

BY TANYA THOMPSON

COPYRIGHT ©2014 TANYA THOMPSON

TO CONTACT THE AUTHOR PLEASE VISIT

TANYATHOMPSONBOOKS.COM

This is a true story. I've changed three names—two of which should be pretty damn obvious—and I've also skewed a minor time line to protect someone I hold dear, but the alterations make no discernable difference to the tale.

You'll find copies of the newspaper and magazine articles mentioned in the book at my website: tanyathompsonbooks.com

When you start thinking, "This is too outrageous to be true," you really do just need to go read the news articles at my site.

FOREWORD

When it was over, my favorite quote made it into all the newspapers. The detective said, "I was dealing with a mastermind."

Oh god, who doesn't want to be called a mastermind?

He said, "This girl has left in her wake a group of professionals." He was talking about the FBI, Interpol, the DEA, INS, a panel of twelve psychologists and psychiatrists, the ACLU, Ron Howard, almost—but not quite—the United States Congress, and finally a couple of sheriff's departments.

I'd been busy.

He said, "I don't believe a normal 15-year-old girl in America pulled this off," and he called me a genius.

I put the newspaper to my lips to kiss the word.

Then he said I needed psychiatric help.

Well, that wasn't nice but it was probably true.

The journalists referred to me as a dark-haired beauty, which was appreciated, but there was no higher flattery than mental brilliance, even if it did come with instability.

I had been trying for years to be recognized as brilliant, but I was capable of some extraordinary acts of stupidity that undermined my efforts.

WOLF MEADOWS

The very night before I ran away to confound the authorities, I was acting moronic.

It was 2:00 a.m. and I had left my family sleeping to hitchhike the thirty miles to Wolf Meadows. Before I left Tennessee for Dallas, I wanted to see if the stories were true. The eighteenth-century mansion in Shelbyville was said to be too haunted to enter, and I had a reputation for insolence in the face of danger, so no one would take me.

Months before, I'd gone to see the famed Chapel Hill Ghost Lights. For hours I sat with three friends on the side of the road, looking over the railroad tracks, hoping to see a decapitated signal man searching the tracks for his head. In the boredom, I lost mine and became condescending, stalking down the tracks shouting, "I've got your head," trying to make him light his lantern and come have a look. Certain that a blue light was swinging in the distance and getting closer, my companions flipped to screaming. I didn't see it, and nothing I said could persuade them to stay and show it to me either.

It took a week's worth of promises to convince them I wouldn't taunt any more ghosts, but once on the porch of Wartrace's Walking Horse Hotel, I proved myself a liar trying to pet an ethereal horse they all shrieked was there.

I had to swear and swear again I wouldn't antagonize the Bell Witch, but the thrill of being at her grave after dark proved too irresistible, and I tried to call her up by claiming to be a Bell heir. I didn't think the witch believed it, but something certainly chased my friends out of the cemetery.

After two months of such late-night supernatural nonsense, all that remained to be seen in Tennessee was Wolf Meadows and Old New Hope Church.

And no one wanted to contemplate me at Wolf Meadows after dark.

But once at Old New Hope Church, my friends decided this too had been a bad idea and they wouldn't tell me what the legend was, convinced I would break into the church and try to carry off the New Hope Bible.

Years later, I heard it couldn't be done. The book would either become too heavy to hold, or it would mysteriously vanish only to reappear at the pulpit. And, of course, anyone who managed to leave the church with it suffered a grisly death.

If they had told me, I might only have laughed.

I wasn't so much sacrilegious as certain everyone else was wrong. There were a lot of things that made no sense to me as they were explained.

I was nine years old the first time I encountered fervent Southern religion. I'd been invited to Sunday service with a friend and listened skeptically as a Baptist preacher told a long story about the love of Jesus, the point of which was to say, "No person can stand before the image of Christ and say, 'I hate you, Jesus.'"

He was emphatic, "It *can not* be done."

He told about one man's attempt to look upon the crucified image and repeat the words three times. The man managed the first blasphemous sentence, but broke down on the second attempt. The preacher boomed, "It can **not** be done."

When the service ended and the preacher went to stand at the door to shake hands with the departing congregants, I went before the empty pulpit and looked up at the tortured figure of Christ on the Cross. I was a little apprehensive because I didn't want to cry and make a fool of myself. I had nothing against Christ, but I needed to confirm if what the preacher had said was true, because it just didn't sound right.

I said, "I hate you, Jesus." And when that went okay, I said again, "I hate you, Jesus." Then, somewhat cringing and waiting for disaster, I whispered, "I hate you, Jesus." I was afraid maybe the last one didn't count, so to make certain, one more time, "I hate you, Jesus."

The preacher was wrong and I earnestly thought he should know so as not to embarrass himself with that story again.

He did not take it well.

I was pulled into a pew for an agonizing thirty-minute confrontation that quickly had me in tears when the preacher said, "Maybe your lack of faith is why your brother just died."

So, yeah, I might have hauled off with the New Hope Bible. But I wasn't the one that burnt either Old New Hope Church or Wolf Meadows to the ground. Both were still standing the night before I ran away.

I saw them for myself, but I saw the last one by myself. I knew there were not enough oaths under heaven to get my superstitious friends to trust me again, and I didn't trust any of them enough to tell them that time was pressing and I really needed to see the place soon. I'd put off going alone until the last night in the hopes they'd come around, but Wolf Meadows was Shelbyville's own home-town terror—a haunted mansion where acts too despicable to discuss had been committed, a place so cursed you could only approach it in a fast car with a competent driver because no one could look upon the place for longer than a minute before going mad with fear.

It sounded positively enchanting. There was absolutely no way I was running away to Dallas without seeing it.

It was mid-September when I went and the night was cool. I had my hands half hidden in the long sleeves of a sweater, considering the mile-long drive that led to the mansion. The city had been granted possession of the avenue and named it Steward Road, but it was nothing more than the driveway to the house. Cedars, hickories, and oaks grew heavy over the lane, turning it black, and I'd come without a flashlight. There were crickets and, if I strained, maybe cows shuffling around in the dark, but nothing that would keep me from entering. I walked the length of the drive, stopping occasionally to listen, and then I paused once more at the last bend to study the dark roof in the field ahead.

It was only the two trees in front of Wolf Meadows that anyone would talk about. I'd been told you could see chain marks cutting into the bark. Those that dared discuss the place said that when it had been used as a home for the mentally handicapped, children had been shackled to the oaks and you could still hear them howling at the moon.

But there was no moon out this night, and standing at the chain link gate, I couldn't see the scars. The sign said *No Trespassing*, but then, didn't they always? I stepped around the gate and over the falling remnants of fence to enter the yard and stand with my back to one of the oaks while I considered the house.

Red brick towered overhead to a peaked balcony jutting out of the attic, and then, just below it, there was another balcony with French doors on the second floor. Brick and stone steps led to a deep recessed entrance, but nothing of it could be seen as it lay in the shadow of the second floor. The place was divided through the middle by this stack of doors, and to either side were large rooms with double windows. The glass wasn't broken, but the place appeared abandoned. The upstairs had no curtains and the downstairs had damaged screens that blocked seeing further inside without light.

I crept around the outside perimeter to check for cars parked in the back, but it was empty. I felt certain I was alone.

I returned to the trees and ran my hands over the bark feeling for the cuts, straining my eyes in the dark to see, but if the trees had been scarred, they had healed.

I looked back to the house. It was eerie. It was big and dark and sitting scary at the end of a mile-long drive. I wasn't certain I wanted to get any closer, but I was moving forward regardless. Up the six steps to the stone landing, peering into the gloom of the recess, sliding one foot forward and then another, hands out in front of me, searching the air for something solid while playing a horrible scene in my head of someone grabbing my wrist. Despite the vivid images in my mind, I kept moving on until finally touching the double doors.

No one I knew had been brave enough to leave the security of their car, much less enter the yard where ghost children were known to wail, and I'd heard no tale of anyone daring to enter the house, but having come so far, I had to see if the doors would open. The handle twisted and the first door gave, but it was tight. I put my hip into it and threw it wide into the hall. Standing on the sill, I couldn't think of a reason to enter, but I was waiting and listening, smelling something old in the air. I'd smelled it before, the scent of decaying newspapers, books, and wallpaper, and aged wood, too, throwing off decades of life under cracking varnish.

I wasn't intending to cross over the threshold, but I couldn't seem to turn away either. I hadn't so much changed my mind as simply carried on, putting my back to the second door, and then slipping into the hall. The faintest light from a window on the side of the house revealed a double opening to my right, and I just kept moving forward even though I knew I shouldn't.

Gliding one foot and then the other across the wood floors, hands out to explore the air, I was edging through the arch. Then keeping to the wall, I was running my fingers over the cracked wallpaper, the cuff of my sweater catching on ripped bits, pulling at the torn paper, tearing it further until it sprang loose from the knit with a tiny flick.

I was nearly in the corner when I heard, "Who are you?"

11

Oh. Good. God. I couldn't breathe. Breathing would require moving, and any movement would lead to running; running would lead to screaming, and screaming in a haunted house was bad.

He asked, "What are you doing?"

Whimpering, but silently. Too terrified to move yet.

Behind me in the dark, springs were creaking free of pressure and someone was getting to their feet.

"What do you want?"

To leave. Leaving now. Casually like nothing is following.

The voice was old, "Have you taken anything?"

Not talking to you. Leaving. Just heading for the door.

Shuffling steps were so very close, "I asked, who are you?"

I felt the air move past my face. He'd reached to stop me but it was utterly black and he'd missed. I picked up the pace. No time to be dignified, but I wasn't running. Running would break into panic.

Out the door and across the stone landing, and then the shout, "Hey!"

No time to chat. I was moving fast down the stairs and into the weeds.

"Now hold on there," he scurried after me and I broke for the gate.

"Wait right there."

And I did, my hand and sweater all caught up in the fence. I was fighting with the chain links for freedom, and he was coming, nearly on me, throwing me into a panic until I ripped free and dashed for the cover of the tree-lined road. Dragging loose yarn through the

12

gravel, blood was streaming down my wrist, soaking my hand, dripping from my fingers to leave a guilty trail to the road.

Running Away

I hadn't gained much by going to Wolf Meadows. I'd not seen chain marks in the trees or heard any wolf children howling, but I learned that a lack of cars did not guarantee solitude. I also came away with a rather horrific-looking, three-inch gash that started at my wrist and sliced down my forearm. It was an unfortunate addition to my image when I had plans to present myself in Dallas as cultured and sophisticated, like the women I had seen in a documentary on Neiman Marcus. It was the world's ultimate luxury store where the clients sat on velvet couches while the fashions were paraded before them in private shows. I was certain none of those ladies would have been caught running through the backwoods, nor had they ever grappled themselves bloody on a chain link fence.

They were far too refined for such nonsense, and I coveted not only their manners but their fur coats and private jets. I had no sense whatsoever of how many necks had been snapped to obtain the one, or any idea of how to afford the other, but I thought a royal title would surely go a long way in securing both. Nothing too immodest though, I merely desired something ambiguous, like countess. Surely no one was keeping up with the world's many countesses. There must be thousands of them, and if one more showed up, no one would notice.

To assume the title and the riches found in Neiman Marcus, I needed to escape Tennessee, dress the part, and sound foreign.

And I'd been faking a British accent for years, so that was hardly a problem. I would change my intonation to entertain myself, often publicly teasing grown men into a fevered passion before retreating behind my father with a face of uncomprehending innocence. And when the opportunity presented itself, I would play proper English to fool adults into selling me alcohol or tickets to R-rated movies.

But that wasn't enough anymore. I'd just turned fifteen and the world was passing me by. I knew it was; I read the national papers and news magazines. So many wonderful things were happening while I sat bored and unchallenged in small town Shelbyville. I loved my family and they loved me, but there was no more time to wait. I had to go.

And they had no idea. I had always presented myself with impassive restraint, so my parents had no reason to suspect my brain was being ripped apart by restless turmoil. They couldn't have guessed I was wandering the highway after midnight. I didn't show my discontent and I was careful to hide the games I played when they weren't looking.

They made their living selling ceramics at arts and crafts shows and had been selling my creations right beside their own since I was eleven. It was seldom I made less than five-hundred dollars in a month, and I spent most of it on clothes and cosmetics. It was 1985, but I didn't dress like Madonna or any other teenager. At twelve, I had decided the only dignified color was black, but I wasn't Goth either. I attained my sense of fashion from older movies; my goal was to look classic.

It was the night after visiting Wolf Meadows, and I was on the highway again. It was past midnight and I was dressed in a black cocktail dress with a full-length fur coat I had purchased the week before. I had just broken into my parents' safe, so in my purse was a thousand dollars.

I had very little plan except to go to Dallas and declare myself a countess. But first I needed to hitchhike to the Nashville Airport, and it wasn't going well. The night was exceptionally black, and, because of my dark clothes, I was uncertain if any of the five cars that had passed had seen me. I had been walking for thirty minutes when it occurred to me I needed to be more aggressive, so I stood half in the lane of the oncoming headlights.

Blue and red lights swirled across the top and the siren squawked a quick warning.

"Curses," I thought, but then, "I can handle it. I've handled worse." I raced for the driver's door, effusing in my English accent, "Oh, thank god. I am so glad to see you. I thought I was going to be left in this wilderness to die."

The sheriff's deputy asked, "Ma'am, what are you doing out here?"

Still gushing, I carried on breathlessly, "I had the most horrible tiff with my husband and demanded he let me out of the car. I didn't think he actually would and he hasn't returned."

"Well, let's get you back to the station and see what we can do."

I rode in the backseat of the cruiser thinking I'd be known as the thirty-minute runaway rather than the Counterfeit Countess.

16

At the sheriff's department, I threw my fur coat over the arm of a chair and sank down beside it, crossing my legs, letting the split in the dress expose my thigh and reveal a thin line of stocking lace. "I cannot thank you enough for rescuing me," I was still pouring out gratitude. "If you would just call me a cab, I will stop being such a nuisance."

"Whoa, hold on there, ma'am, I don't even know your name."

"Oh … of course … forgive me," I was drawing out the apology because I didn't know what name I planned to use either. I reached for one of the many I'd used before, "I'm Amanda Forster."

"And what were you doing out on the highway at this hour?"

Ducking my head, I forced a blush. "It is terribly embarrassing, but my husband and I had an awful row. I didn't think he would actually stop the car when I told him to." It occurred to me I was not wearing a wedding band, and before he asked, he needed to know I had no identification. I clasped my empty ring fingers, saying, "I was so mad, I threw all my jewelry at him, then I threw my passport and driver's license. I just threw it all at his face and told him to go. Wasn't that silly?"

"Yes, ma'am, that was a little …" he couldn't bring himself to say it. Then something else occurred to him. "How were you going to pay for a cab?"

"Well, I'm not foolish," I smiled to pull him in. "I didn't throw my *cash* at him," and we laughed together.

"Where are you from?"

"Tanzania."

He furrowed his brows. "Transylvania?"

17

"Oh, deputy," I giggled, "you are so funny."

He seemed pleased, then confused, and he asked again, "Where are you from?"

"Tanzania."

"Really?"

I could see he'd never heard of it. "It's right next to Mozambique."

But that didn't seem to clarify much either. He asked, "What language do they speak … there?"

"Swahili."

One eye opened a little wider. "Say something for me in … that language. What is it again?"

"Swahili," I smiled. Then holding his eyes, I purred out the words, "Orrysay orfay omorrowtay."

"Isn't that something?" He shook his head with wonder then picked up the phone. I listened as he woke up the owner of a nearby cab company, explaining there was a woman in great need. The cab owner wouldn't drive to Shelbyville, but if the deputy would bring me the thirty miles to his business, he'd get me to the Nashville airport.

I implored, "Oh, please do."

And the deputy smiled, "I can tell you haven't been in the South very long. We are known for our hospitality." Then as he was leading me out of the station to his car, he requested, "Say something in Swahili again for the boys."

And I called over my shoulder to the other deputies, "It'say eenbay unfay!"

~~~~~~

18

My night with the police had not ended there. The cab broke down on the way to the airport, and I was transported to the Smyrna police station to play the same game a second time. But no one was too concerned with what had happened in Smyrna. The report listing me as a runaway was filed with the Shelbyville police, and it was the local police that dropped my picture on the desk of the sheriff's deputy. He went pale and tried to cover my smiling face. He started shouting at the officer, but she had already seen his guilt. She demanded he speak, that he tell her what he knew, but he shouted louder, forcing her into the hall before slamming the door.

The sheriff was called.

It took an hour to reason with the deputy behind closed doors. When they finally emerged, both looked weak with disbelief, but there was no getting around it, they had to confess what had been done.

When my father showed up, the deputy insisted, "But she spoke Swahili. I know it was a foreign language."

"Pig Latin," my father told them. "She speaks fluent Pig Latin."

They tracked me to the Smyrna Police Department and then to another cab company. I was last seen at the Nashville Airport, but no one guessed I was already in Dallas.

DALLAS

Sometimes I think there is something slightly wrong with me, and not in the way most people suspect. I lack a proper sense of fear. I'm hard to scare but easy to startle, and I'm not entirely fearless. For instance, I want no part of bungee jumping, skydiving, or any other high-altitude scare; but things on the ground have to get pretty extreme for my heart rate to change. I have a difficult time recognizing danger when walking into it. Before my time in Dallas was over, a mafia henchman was going to hold a gun to my head, and that did not so much frighten as annoy me. So, even though I had no plan, I was not alarmed or concerned. Even though this was going to be the biggest act I had ever put on, I intended to play it as I always had—pure improvisation, all on impulse, with little more known than I would be playing the part of a countess.

In the late afternoon, I had a taxi drop me at an address just outside of Dallas, and then when he was gone, I started walking along the highway. "I'll be lost," I started concocting the first act in my performance. "I'll be the lost countess." It sounded quite mysterious.

When a man stopped to ask if I needed help, I graciously accepted and got into his car. "I'm afraid I am a bit turned around."

"Where were you trying to go?"

"Well," I looked over the green lawns passing outside the windows, "I was supposed to be in Egypt."

The conversation wasn't going to make any more sense as we moved further along either. He took me home and called his church. "She thinks if she gets to Egypt, whoever is looking for her will find her." After a bit of silence on his end, he agreed with the preacher, "No, we can't have that. I'll bring her right over."

It was Wednesday night and the Baptist church in Plano was packed with hundreds of congregants. I was in the preacher's large office but he couldn't make any more sense of me than the motorist had, so they went out and got Mike, a retired FBI agent.

As Mike and the preacher entered the office, I was explaining to a deacon, "I just need to get to Egypt, then I'm sure they will find me."

Mike took a chair opposite me and wanted to know, "How are they going to find you?"

"Well," I stopped to consider it, "I don't know. They were expecting me, so surely they will look."

Mike settled into a thinking stare, taking in the fur coat draped over the arm of the couch, the black cocktail dress, the high heels, and the accent. I couldn't tell his age but I thought he was in his forties. What I did recognize was he was serious, and his eyes were critical, not at all like the preacher who worried about my soul rather than the facts. Mike said, "Let's start again. What is your name?"

"Constance."

"Your full name."

I hadn't thought that far ahead. I paused for the briefest moment to think. I was thinking about my father. His first marriage had been to a Bolivian, and when he gave her full name, it seemed to run on forever. It was gloriously foreign and exotic. As Mike waited to hear my name, I was trying to remember how my father had accounted for them all. Some of her names had come from maternal and paternal grandparents, and then something was from her mother, and maybe more from her father, and lastly she'd taken the surname of my father. If I hoped to pass as foreign, I thought I would need at least four names to be taken seriously.

I started stringing them together, "Countess Constance Anna Marie Tanya Mitchell."

I dropped countess on them like it were nothing, added my own name because I liked it, and then practically undid myself by choosing the last name of the family dog. The dog was Martha Mitchell, named after the wife of John Mitchell, President Nixon's Attorney General. The dog had come into our family a year old and already named, and I still have no idea what I was thinking when I borrowed her surname, but when you're making things up as you go along, these things tend to happen.

Mike asked me to say my name again and I nearly laughed. I hoped I remembered the order. "Countess Constance Anna Marie Tanya Mitchell."

"You're a countess?"

"Yes."

"Where are you from?"

"I just came from Kenya."

"So, you're Kenyan?" the preacher asked. To Mike he said, "She does sound South African."

"I have been there, too," I acknowledged.

22

"But where are you from?"

I said again, "I just came from Kenya."

Mike asked, "What country issued your passport?"

I looked confused.

"Your passport. You have a passport, don't you?"

I appeared to search my memory, but didn't sound convinced, "I believe so."

"You need a passport to travel."

I nodded my head but said nothing.

Mike was quiet for a moment, then he asked, "Have you seen your passport?"

"Maybe. I don't know."

"How do you travel then?"

"Generally by plane."

Now Mike looked confused.

I offered as though it would clarify something, "Sometimes by car. Once on a boat. And a couple times by rail. But mostly planes."

I didn't know where this fiction was ultimately going, but I had a goal. I wanted to live in Dallas with the title of countess. The only problem was I had not yet learned how to create a legitimate, federally recognized identity, and as it was 1985, there was no readily available information on the topic. Uncertain how to acquire identification, I needed a compelling history to explain why I had none. Every question Mike asked allowed me to give the tale more detail, but so far, he had about as much of a clue as I did how the story was going to proceed.

Mike said, "When you arrived in this country, you would have shown your passport to immigration." And when I gave no indication this had happened, he prompted, "Do you remember giving your passport to immigration?"

"No."

"You don't remember?"

"No."

"Why don't you remember?"

"When you say immigration, I don't know what you mean."

Mike inhaled and the preacher struck out with, "How many countries have you been in?"

"Thirty, maybe more."

Mike sat forward with consternation. It was a far higher number than he was expecting. "You would have gone through immigration at every international airport."

I looked interested to hear it.

Mike tried to make it simple. "Who are the first officials you meet when you enter a country?"

"Do you mean the military?"

He leaned farther forward. "What is the first thing you normally do when you get off a plane?"

"I give the valise to the person at the bottom of the stairs."

Mike went rigid and the preacher whispered slow and full of breath, "Oh ... my ... stars."

Mike asked, "What's in the valise?"

"I don't know."

"Okay." He paused to rearrange his thoughts. "*Then* what do you do?"

"Generally, I get into a car."

Suddenly it was clear to Mike. "You've been traveling by private plane." He sat back thinking he was finally getting a handle on it. "But you'd still have to pass through immigration." And when I kept my expression blank, he considered something else. "How big are the airports?"

I looked quizzical.

"How big? How many runways? How many buildings?"

"Well, only one runway and there are seldom any buildings."

The preacher declared with astonishment, "Clandestine landing strips."

~~~~~~

Mike needed a moment away to organize his thoughts, and then, "When I return, we're going to start all over again."

After Mike left the room, the preacher wanted to talk to me about my soul. "Are you a Christian?"

I said with the same doe-eyed innocence I had been using from the start, "I have been."

He pulled back. "Have you been something else?"

"A couple times I was Buddhist, once a Hindu, and twice a Jew, though mostly a Christian, if not agnostic."

He was aghast. He needed a moment too, but there wasn't a minute to spare if he was going to save me from that blasphemous list. "What are you now?"

I smiled and granted, "While I am in your company, I will be a Christian."

He was breathless, dropping to his knees before me, already asking, "Will you pray with me?"

"Why, yes, of course, if you like," but I was pushing back into the couch in a bid for distance, hoping it was not as it appeared, praying all decorum was not about to be lost.

But the preacher took my hands and pulled me forward onto the floor, both of us now facing each other on our knees. He had tears in his eyes wanting to know, "Have you accepted Jesus as your Lord and Savior?"

He was so earnest and I was stunned, overwhelmed with embarrassment for us both. I was trying to figure out how we had come to be on the floor on our knees, because whatever mistake had brought us to this, I wanted to be certain to never make it again. I went with the answer I thought he wanted, the one I hoped would get us off the floor. I said optimistically, "Yes."

"*When*? When did you accept Jesus as your Lord and Savior?"

Oh Jesus Christ, my silent mind snapped without any concept of irony. He sounded as though he was pleading for the answer, and my calm ability to lie was floundering on his emotions. I struggled for a response, searching my brain for what it actually meant, what I would be admitting, accepting someone as my lord and savior. Something about it sounded just a little too subservient for my rebellious spirit to accept. I finally reacted with a noise somewhere between a laugh and a whimper.

His shoulders fell with his heavy exhale. "You *haven't* accepted Jesus as your Lord and Savior." He was devastated.

Afraid I was about to be made to, I assured a little too enthusiastically, "No, I have, I have. I just don't remember when. Ha," I laughed somewhat hysterically. "So many acceptances, it's hard to keep track. I accept him every day!" and then another whimpering laugh.

I looked around the room. Where was cool, removed Mike? But the preacher put his hand on top of my head and forced it down. He was praying for my soul. And he had a great many concerns. I stared at the carpet wondering when it was going to end, telling myself I needed to figure out this religion thing before I went any further, promising I would never make light of it again in front of someone who could put me on my knees.

<center>~~~~~~~</center>

Eventually Mike reentered, and the preacher let me up.

I felt pretty well humiliated, and was thinking I, too, could have used a moment, but Mike didn't register anything odd about us getting off the floor.

Mike had a new approach. He wanted to take everything backwards from the moment his fellow congregant offered me assistance. "How did you come to be there? Where were you just before you were walking beside the highway?"

"In a car."

"Good. In a car. Who was driving?"

"I don't know."

"Okay, that's fine; we'll come back to it. How did you get from the car to the side of the road?"

"I got out of the car."

Mike was getting the hang of how the whole exchange was going to proceed. "Why did you get out of the car?"

"I was told to."

And in that exact minimalist manner, we traveled all the way back to Kenya. It had been quite a journey. I explained I had spent the past six months in palatial home overlooking the Savanna, and when it was time to move to Egypt, I was given a valise.

Mike asked, "Do you always change homes with a valise?"

"From my earliest memories, I have always travelled with one."

"Is it the same valise you arrive with?"

"No, it was never obviously the same one."

When pressed, I admitted I was being escorted by a man named Alistair who was meant to see me off at a Kenyan airstrip but had instead boarded the plane. We flew to another landing strip, and then to another before driving to a helicopter in a field. Alistair hadn't explained. He had simply taken the valise, and then pressed hundreds of US dollars into my hands.

Mike looked in my handbag and saw it contained the bills and lipstick, but nothing else. He asked, "Did Alistair appear nervous?"

"I suppose, now that you mention it, he did seem a little anxious."

"You didn't question what was happening?" the preacher interjected.

I considered it as though such an action had never once occurred to me, and then answered, "No."

The helicopter flew over the ocean and deposited me on a ship. From my description, Mike thought it sounded like an oil tanker. I stayed locked in solitude in a little cabin for what seemed like two weeks. Though Mike asked, I could give no details about the ship or its crew as I was never allowed out of the cabin. When the coast began to show lights, I descended a rope ladder to a waiting boat, and this boat landed on a dark, unpopulated shore. A man was waiting for me with a car and we drove through the night until he told me to get out, leaving me without explanation on the side of the road.

I told the same story over and over, backwards and forwards without confusion. And while I could give details about the scenery and weather, I could offer no specifics such as license plate numbers or names.

"Extraordinary," the preacher declared.

Mike showed neither belief nor disbelief. "Who were you staying with in Kenya?"

I paused and looked away to make it appear I was lying, mumbling, "I don't know."

The preacher jumped in saying, "But you know the address."

Even more uncomfortable, I answered, "No." Such details would obviously be known, but they could also be confirmed, and that had to be avoided. It was best to let them think I was too afraid to say.

The preacher was bewildered, but Mike showed nothing, he merely asked, "Do you know anyone's name from Kenya?"

"Alistair."

"He's long gone," the preacher announced.

"Anyone else?"

I covered my mouth and shook my head.

"You stayed six months in this house, and you learned only one name?" Mike was harsh. He had at last decided to show an opinion about my story.

The devil in me smiled. Mike hadn't thrown his skepticism on the story as a whole, just the small part that I didn't know anyone's name. In doing so, he began to accept the bigger lie. I knew he wasn't convinced, not entirely, but it was a start.

I had my eyes fixed in my lap when Mike asked, "Is Alistair the only person you interacted with for six months?"

"No."

"Who else?"

"A man."

"What was his name?"

I stopped breathing, looked away, and barely whispered, "I don't know."

"Then how did you address him? What did you call him?" Mike thought he had me.

30

I tried to make it apparent I was tearing my brain apart searching for an answer that would appease. I practically smiled when it occurred to me. My face lit up with hope that it would be believed. I said, "I called him master."

~~~~~~

I had no idea what I had just implied. I was fifteen and had never heard of submissives, slaves, gimps, or dominatrixes. I had read a couple fantasy novels with masters of magic, but I was mostly thinking of the martial arts where the respected sensei might be called something like Master Musashi.

Of all the things, I had not meant to turn my tale into one of human trafficking and prostitution.

I did not understand why the preacher sighed out, "No, child," and appeared distraught.

I couldn't account for Mike's abrupt discomfort, or his shift to gentle inquisition. He was staring at my left wrist. He'd been preoccupied with it for some time. He said, "Let me see," and held out his hand.

The fence at Wolf Meadows had left a three-inch fresh cut straight down my forearm from my wrist. It was bloody red and ghastly to see, but as far as I knew, the only way to suicidally slit your wrists was from side to side, so the injury running down my arm seemed entirely innocent.

In under a minute, I had gone from merely confounding to fantastically tragic, and my smiling assurance that, "It looks worse

31

than it is," did little to dissuade Mike's interest. I flipped my hand to get it out of sight.

Mike asked, "When did you do that?"

"Three nights ago."

His next question, "What did you do it with?" did not register as *how did you do it to yourself?*

I answered, "A nail," and the preacher sighed so sadly, I became convinced he was dramatically oversensitive. I said to alleviate his stress, "It didn't hurt. It was just a stray nail in the railing of the ship."

But Mike saw a problem with my explanation. "So you weren't completely confined to a cabin."

Damn it. And I knew I looked like I was thinking damn it, too. I smiled guilty contrition. "I convinced one of the crew to let me out to walk the deck, but I promised not to tell."

"A nail in the railing," Mike repeated. "Don't you think someone would have removed it?"

"I'm sure they did after I discovered it."

But it was clear Mike wasn't buying it. Of all the things I had dropped on them in the last two hours, I could not fathom why he would fixate on my wrist. It was, as far as I could tell, entirely inconsequential, yet it was the point Mike was going to come back to time and again.

"How old are you?"

"Twenty-three."

"How did you cut your wrist?"

"On a nail."

"How do you know you're twenty-three?" And when I look puzzled, Mike asked, "Have you seen your birth certificate?"

"No."

"Then how do you know?"

"I was told."

"What did you cut your wrist with?"

"A nail in the railing."

"You've always been addressed as countess?"

"Yes."

"When did you cut your wrist?"

"Three nights ago."

"Where were you before Kenya?"

"China."

"And before that?"

"Germany."

And before that South Africa, and before that Brazil, and between each, "How did you cut your wrist?"

"On a nail."

"Can you tell me a single name from any of the places you've lived in your twenty-three years?"

I let my eyes float slowly around the room, and then answered with an unconvincing, "No."

"Most of the homes you've described staying in were large. They would have had staff."

My silence forced Mike to prompt, "*Yes?*"

"Yes."

"You never learned any of their names?"

I blushed hard and let my eyes stray again. The act was an unfamiliar paradox. To make these lies work, I had to look like a bad liar.

Mike pressed, "You must have heard them talking to each other."

I slowly shook my head to deny it.

"You never heard them talking? You never heard them call out to one another?"

"No."

"Why not?"

I gaped back dumbfounded.

"Were they mute? How could you not have heard them speak to each other?"

I made an obvious show of hunting for a plausible answer, and then answered weakly, "I seldom left my room."

Mike stared at my wrist and thought about it. "So, staying alone in the cabin on the ship would have been familiar."

"The environment was different."

"I imagine you got quite depressed," the preacher said.

That was an emotion I had never experienced or imagined. I responded brightly, "No, not at all."

"Explain the cut on your wrist," Mike said.

"It was dark. I didn't see the nail in the railing."

"It didn't bother you to be alone?"

"No."

"You're accustomed to it?"

I gave an uncertain "Yes," as though I was afraid of the trap Mike was laying.

"You make it sound as though the only people you have spoken to in your adult life are the various hosts you've lived with."

My expression acknowledged that this was an unfortunate absurdity, but one I was going to have to stick with.

"In the twenty-nine countries you've lived, you never once heard your host's name?"

I rolled my lips between my teeth to indicate my mouth was sealed and shook my head.

Mike found another opening. "How did other people address your host? By what name?"

I made a silent "Oh" with my mouth as though I had been irrefutably caught and recognized only the truth would pass. I nearly answered but changed my mind, and then almost said something else before shaking my head and deciding firmly, "Master. They were known to everyone as master."

~~~~~~

Two hours in and I was a suicidal submissive when what I had really been going for was more along the lines of mysterious smuggler. But I didn't know that yet. I still thought I was successfully fabricating the image of a naive woman protecting dangerous allies.

I would occasionally try to give the impression of bringing Mike's questioning to a close by saying, "All I really need is to get to Egypt. If you could just help me arrange a flight ..." but Mike's expression would always turn pained and I'd trail off while the preacher emphatically shook his head.

Finally, the preacher informed me, "Alistair went to a great deal of trouble to get you clear of that life and we're not going to send you back to it."

"Even if we could," Mike added.

At the end of four hours, I went home with a member of the church, and the next day, Mike took me to the FBI.

We were in a front interview room with two agents. Mike outlined my story, and then I answered the same questions as the night before.

The agents admitted they had known for some time that white women were being smuggled around the globe, but I was the first evidence they had seen.

It was clear that everyone was fixated on the word master, and as it held their interest so keenly, I stopped trying to make it obvious I was lying. But it was going to be years before the sexual use of the word was explained to me, so in the meantime, I was thinking, "Wow, an international circle of masters smuggling women across the continents." It sounded fascinating. I thought the women must be trained assassins, and if anything, I wished to join them.

There was a master in every country, I assured the FBI.

But it was beyond me to understand why the agents wanted to know if I had sex with the masters. I was insulted, answering with a frown, "No, never."

No one in the room believed me.

But my genuine confusion as to why they would think it made them doubt. "Then, what were you doing with them?" one agent asked.

"Well, certainly not that," but I wouldn't elaborate further.

As I could give no details of a crime, the FBI couldn't investigate. But they took my fingerprints, telling Mike they would run them through the system, and while they were at it, probably send the report to Washington headquarters, and maybe have a little look around, ask a few questions. But ultimately, the agents were of the opinion that this was the sort of thing Interpol should be brought in on. And because of the valise, we should go to the DEA.

OVER THE FALLS

The start of the next week, Mike and I did the whole thing again with the DEA. They took my fingerprints, made a report, and said they'd look into it. But as I wouldn't admit any knowledge of what I was transporting, they couldn't assume it was drugs. They told Mike to come back when it was clear.

The following day, Mike took me back to the church. There was a psychologist waiting to talk. Again, it was the wrist. I was flummoxed as to why it kept coming up.

The psychologist asked, "Do you want to tell me what really happened?"

"I promise you, it was a nail. I didn't see it in the dark, and ran my arm over it."

I could think of no way to explain what had happened any more convincingly unless I changed my story by adding a chain link fence to the boat.

"You're safe here. You can tell me. We're alone. No one else has to know."

I looked suddenly troubled, but it wasn't for any reason the psychologist suspected. I took a breath, he thought I was about to confess, but it was a breath of patience, because I needed patience if this was going to continue. I said, "Thank you, but I sincerely do not care in the least who knows. It was a stray nail in the railing."

From his briefcase, he pulled out the Rorschach inkblot test, and I could not stop myself from laughing.

"Why do you find this funny?"

"Am I going to be labeled insane over a nail?"

"Do you think the nail is the issue?"

"Is it not?"

"What do you see in this card?"

After the first card that looked like a butterfly, I steadfastly contended, "I see nothing."

He thought I was being obstinate.

Next he handed me paper and pen, saying, "We are going to do a word association exercise. Write down the first word that comes to mind. If I say salt, what is the first word that enters your mind? Write it down." Halfway through, he was quite impressed with how fast I was responding, but then when it was over, he saw I had only written down exactly what he had said.

I defended myself, "The word you said would be the first word that would come to mind." Now he knew beyond doubt I was being difficult.

"You're not going to tell me how you cut your wrist?"

"It was a nail."

I went straight to a night admission at the psychiatric hospital.

~~~~~

On the third day under observation, I was sitting on the side of the bed, my hands over my eyes, saying with exasperation bordering on despair, "It was a nail."

The psychiatrist said, "One more chance, and then I'm leaving. I'm going to petition the court to continue holding you. You'll be moved to the state mental hospital. It won't be pleasant."

I was racking my brain trying to figure out how a nail injury could look so significantly different from a chain link fence injury that everyone except me could see it.

I couldn't fathom, and no one was whispering even a hint about their suspicions. I was playing twenty-three and worldly, so it was probably assumed that I knew the most efficient way to slit your wrist was down the vein, and it was probably suspected that I wasn't outright denying or admitting an attempt at suicide because I was ashamed, or was in denial, or in some other psychological quandary, but the reality was I didn't have a clue. I had only just turned fifteen and none of this had been covered in ninth grade.

Hollywood had taught me that suicide was done with razor sharp precision across your wrist, and I had a savage cut down my arm. To my mind, no one would deliberately scar themselves like that, so it was clearly an accident.

It was the cause of the accident that was at issue. Apparently boats did not have stray nails in the railings. I didn't know, but I still argued with the psychiatrist like I did. "You're not a carpenter, yet you're going to tell me that railings are not assembled with nails. How do you know that? Why would you tell me they're not when I have seen for myself that they are?"

He wouldn't explain. He only warned, "Last chance. Tell me how you cut yourself."

But I had never been one to change a story. I'd stick with it to the bitter, twisted end, and before it was over, I'd wear everyone else down into believing it through sheer stubborn consistency.

I threw a hand up in resignation, telling the psychiatrist, "It was still a nail."

And he left without saying a word.

~~~~~~

It went exactly as the psychiatrist threatened. The judge sent me to Wichita Falls State Mental Hospital, and, as was warned, it wasn't pleasant.

The place was a square grid of thirty-odd brick buildings. Most were residential halls, long sprawling two- and three-story structures arranged around treeless green lawns. It almost could have passed for a college campus, except most of the windows were barred and it lacked any sense of external life. Expressionless faces were watching from the windows, but no one was on the grass. The vibe was so subdued it felt threatening.

It was built in the 1920s and retained little glimpses of another era when electroshock therapy and lobotomies were acceptable. During admission, I saw leather restraints, harnesses, and straight jackets; then later, I took a shower in a wide open, tiled hall with two

41

cast iron tubs that had once been used for cold shock therapy. The place had not been modernized, so the threats remained.

I was put into an adult ward with two dozen other females. Most of them were schizophrenics, a few were manic-depressives, and all of them seemed tipped for violence. But worse, a majority of the women were round-the-clock shrieking maniacs.

The screaming started on my arrival and never stopped. It was constant and of every variety. Hysterical screaming. Angry screaming. Tear-filled accusations led to monosyllabic screaming. Huge men in white coats would wrestle someone to the floor, and while a nurse injected them with sedatives, other screamers on the sidelines would cheer and curse and throw whatever wasn't bolted down until someone else got restrained. Then everyone would scream some more.

I was pressed into a corner thinking this was not nearly as funny as I imagined it would be. Having arrived late on Friday, it was going to be three nights before the doctors I had to convince I was sane came back to work, and by Sunday night, I was pretty certain I had been sent to hell.

When Monday arrived, I had already woken up to a woman sitting next to me with a pair of scissors saying, "Your hair is real pretty." So, when I was called before the panel of twelve psychologists and psychiatrists, I was careful not to pitch my voice too high or out of control like everyone else.

They sat on one side of a long table and I sat alone in the center of the room.

42

We went through my whole story as Mike, the FBI, and the DEA had heard it, and at no point did anyone express skepticism.

At the end they asked, "Do you know why you're here?"

I was not about to bring up the nail. I went with, "I'm not entirely certain."

"You want to take a guess?"

"No, not particularly."

"You want to tell us why not?"

It was the only earnest sentiment I would willingly share with them, "A person who goes wildly stabbing in the dark might stab herself, and I have never been inclined to cripple myself."

They said, "Very well then, you can leave."

Oh thank god. I was smiling relief and said sincerely, "Thank you."

A little too sincerely, so they felt the need to clarify, "You can leave the room."

~~~~~~

Legally they were only allowed to hold me for two weeks before the court required a formal diagnosis of insanity to continue detaining me. I had already spent three days at the first hospital and another three at the Falls, which left the psychiatric panel eight days to determine if I was sane.

Just minutes free of the initial interview, I fell into conflict with one of the psychologists.

I had refused the physical exam required upon admittance, and I continued to reject the psychologist's demands that I submit. She called the men in white coats, and while they stood outside her office door, she informed me, "You have a choice: you can either walk to the clinic or be carried."

"That is not a choice."

"Of course it is. Now which will it be?"

I chose to walk. My wrist was again the focus of interest. The doctor clucked over it, "You poor thing. This is a terrible place for someone as young as you to be." He looked at my other wrist and said, "I'm glad there is only one."

I laughed, "I can't imagine what events would lead to this happening twice."

And he sighed, "We never can and I hope you never do."

Goodness, it seemed everyone in Texas was intensely melodramatic.

The psychologist was in an angry drama that saw her slamming her hands down on the desk. She'd lost all patience with me, commanding on my return, "For the last time, the truth!"

"It was a nail."

"I'm not going to listen to your lies. Get out of my office!"

The next morning, I was woken with a rough shake and opened my eyes to someone's face just an inch from mine, shouting like a Marine drill sergeant, "What is your name? What is your name? Full name now!"

He had me by the arms and I gave him what he wanted in a rush, "Tanya Thompson." Then backing up the wall to escape, made the correction, "Constance Mitchell."

With a smile and a wink, he turned and left.

The aftermath was a shocking quiet calm. I looked over the room, taking in the white stone walls, the bars over the windows, and then, at the open door, was the psychologist. I was full of contempt. "Bloody hell, is this how you people amuse yourself?"

"Tanya?"

"No, Constance."

"Who is Tanya?"

"A sister. A friend. Someone I know."

"Then why did you give her name?"

"We look very similar and I've used her name before." And when she rolled her eyes in disbelief, I asked in defense, "If you woke to some unknown man on top of you wanting your name, would you give your real one? Well, of course *you* might, but then you are rather witless."

We didn't become any greater of friends as the days passed.

She demanded, "Why are you so thin?"

But I was stumped to explain it.

"They say you don't eat."

"The food here is different than what I am accustomed."

"You will eat it, or you will be confined to the cafeteria until you do."

After four hours, the mess on my plate was no longer a steaming spread of unidentifiable mush but was instead something congealed and sickening. The men in white left their positions at the exit to come stand beside me and shake their heads. They reached a whispered agreement between themselves and then silently took pity on me, dumping the whole tray in the trash and swearing to the nurse I had eaten.

The next day, the psychologist turned it all around by saying, "Until you tell me the truth about how you cut yourself, you are not allowed to eat. Don't even bother going to the cafeteria because I have instructed them not to feed you."

By evening I was uncomfortably hungry. The woman with the scissors who had thought my hair was pretty pulled me aside to dig bits of bread out of her pockets. She'd collected slices from other patients at the table and then balled them in her fist to shove into hiding. The bread was caked in pocket fluff, and I wasn't that desperate, but it was a touching gesture that sided the patients against the staff. I thanked her for the effort but had to decline.

She granted it wasn't perfect, saying, "Next time, I'll wrap it in a napkin."

The following morning I was starving and started performing physics experiments in my head. I was trying to determine if it was the angle or the depth that betrayed the cut to my wrist had not been a nail but a chain link fence. Again and again, I replayed the dark tangle with the fence in the night, but it had happened so fast I didn't notice the cut until the blood started dripping from my fingers. Instead, I tried to imagine swiping my hand over a railing and how easily the same injury could be done with a nail. I could not find the flaw in my lie.

46

I studied my wrist and had to consider that I was out of my depth. I had to concede that I was dealing with people far more intelligent than I had assumed. Everyone in Texas could see something I couldn't. They were all decades older than me, and some experience gave them insight that I lacked. It was frustrating. I wondered repeatedly if I should just give up and admit my real name, but I was not yet prepared to return home.

The psychologist tried again, her temper barely concealed. "Tell me the truth."

I asked, "About what?"

"Anything."

"The only constant in the universe is change?"

She shouted, "Get out!"

But always later, someone would find me trying to make myself small and unseen in some corner of the corridor, hoping to avoid the violent screaming in the dayroom, waiting for evening when the doors to the bedrooms were unlocked and I could hide from the madness. I'd be escorted back with the explanation the psychologist wanted to talk again.

"I want you to tell me the truth about how you hurt yourself," she said.

"What do you want to hear? If there is a story you prefer, I am prepared at this point to tell it."

"If you don't want my help, get out."

I turned at the door. "Why do you imagine I want your help?"

"Because without it, you're not getting out of here."

Then on Saturday, with my court case pending on Monday, she came in especially to intimidate me. "You either tell me now or, I promise, I will tell the judge you should be kept here indefinitely."

The threat was too big. The first psychiatrist who had threatened to send me to the Falls had seen it through, so I suspected she could to. I didn't want my con to end in a mental institution over something so unimportant. I hated it, everything in me was against it, but I had to relent.

"All right, all right," I huffed in exasperated defeat. "It wasn't a nail."

She sat back instantly happy. Her chin was high with pride, and she smiled, satisfied that she had finally cracked me.

Then I confessed, "It was a chain link fence."

Her face fell, but I was too angry at having been terrorized with indefinite detention to look at her any longer. I started explaining in a fast rambling admission, "There was a section cordoned off on the boat, and I got tangled up in it when I slipped. I'm not accustomed to walking in heels on the high seas. Blessed hell, this seems a lot of fuss for me to keep a promise, but I swore to the man I wouldn't tell anyone that he'd let me into the cargo cage. I wanted to see the birds that had gotten trapped. Some crew members were feeding them bread and I had some to give them too, but then there was a wave, and I fell and my hand went through the fence. I can't even tell you what exactly cut me, but it was a sharp part of the chain link fence. Okay?" Full of hostility, I glared at her. "It was a chain link fence."

Her expression of slack-jawed dismay clenched tight and she pointed at the door, "Out! Out of my sight!"

On Monday, the court heard I was uncooperative. The judge had read to the end of my file and said, "Well, I imagine so. I would be, too."

The state argued the psychologist's opinion that I should be sent back.

The judged flipped through the file again. "There is no indication she suffers from delusions or is a threat to herself or others. It is not a crime to have had a difficult upbringing. I'm letting her go."

FALSE REFUGE

The investigation into my past was being handled by the Collin County Sheriff's Department and primarily by a detective named Rick. While I was detained in the first psychiatric hospital, my details had been run through all of the fifty states' missing persons reports, but the search parameter listed me as a twenty-three-year-old adult, and Tennessee had lost a fifteen-year-old juvenile.

Then from the Falls, Rick received my real name. He ran Tanya Thompson through the same search, but the fates were on my side and no match was made. Seven months later, it would be called a computer glitch.

But for now, Rick was at a loss. He made contact with Interpol. They were anxious to get my file and start a search, but it was going to take a week to send the lost persons forms and then a while longer to fill them in.

While the sheriff's department waited to hear from the various US agencies investigating, no one was too certain what to do with me. I wasn't insane, and although everyone was certain I knew more than I was letting on, no one could guess what it was.

Free from the daily confrontations with the psychologist, I had returned my expression to one of sweet baffled innocence. The sheriff's department wasn't responsible for doing any more than turning me loose on the street, but as all the detectives agreed, "There are people you can do that with, however, she is not one of them."

Rick knew someone would take advantage of me, and unable to abide that, he arranged for me to live with the director of the Dallas/Fort Worth Refugee Agency. The director of the agency was primarily working with Cambodians who had fled the genocide of the Khmer Rouge, but she also assisted Romanians, Bulgarians, and other political refugees that had escaped the Soviet Eastern Bloc. In the confusion of foreigners seeking residence, I was not the only one pretending to be something I wasn't. There was no way Rick could have known when he delivered me to the agency that I would meet another imposter, or that six months later, the Italian posing as a Romanian would threaten to blow his head off.

~~~~~~

Like so many others in Dallas, Tricia had no reason to help me, but she did. As the director of the Dallas/Fort Worth Refugee Agency, she was assisting a fair number of misplaced people, but unlike the others, she invited me into her home. The bungalow wasn't large, but it was newly remodeled and sat in a pleasant middle-class area across from a park and golf course. It was decorated in a style that reflected Tricia — part art deco, part bohemian. In her bedroom was an antique traveling trunk that mesmerized me with its compartments of feather headbands and long strands of beads. It also had a delicate flapper dress that perfectly suited Tricia's blond bobbed hair and slim build. She was in her mid-thirties and comfortable enough with herself to not be bothered by me or my story.

51

From the start, she took me to work with her, giving me a desk and a purpose. I spent my days calling local businesses, arranging job interviews for the agency's unemployed, and occasionally I would be given the keys to the agency's car to get one of them to an appointment.

Tricia didn't think to ask if I knew how to drive, and I didn't mention I never had, so I struck out into Dallas traffic with no previous experience of one-way streets, no idea who had the right-of-way, and far too busy trying to learn the actual mechanics of driving a car to spend any time deciphering the inexplicable road signs. From the start, it was obvious that I was the focus of a great many horns, but they were seldom any louder than the person screaming hysterically in the passenger seat. It seemed the best way to get clear of it all was to go faster, but the traffic in Dallas was relentless, so my rides of chaos tended to sound like one long cacophony of experimental jazz in an Oriental opera.

At our destination, I'd put the car in park, triumphant that we'd escaped all the maniacs on the road, and then look over to my passenger and truly wonder why they couldn't return my elation.

Maintaining a constant impression of round-eyed naivety was not hard, as it was not terribly far from the truth. Most things were new to me. I had been raised in rural Tennessee and now had the freedom of an adult in Dallas. It was assumed I knew the basics of life, or, at the very least, to possess a sense of preservation to keep myself and others safe.

I would repeatedly prove I didn't.

The very first day at the agency, I went with Tricia as she helped a Cambodian family transition into a first world apartment. While Tricia spoke with the husband and dealt with official paperwork in the living room, she asked me to teach the wife how to use the oven. I didn't know myself, so I had to study it before passing on incorrect and incomprehensible instructions through language charades. Two days later, the woman filled the stove with wood, set it on fire, and burned the entire apartment complex to the ground.

The second day, I was left in charge of several Cambodian children while Tricia spoke with their mothers. I gave them paper and crayons, and when they didn't know what to do with them, I told the children to draw pictures of their families. Every one of them drew bodies hanging dead from the trees. Without the sense to take the crayons away, I sat in horrified astonishment as more and more graphic illustrations were laid in my lap until eventually the mothers returned to find their children in a sort of shock, maniacally covering the pages in the blood of red crayons.

The third day, I collected a newly arrived Cambodian family from the Dallas/Fort Worth Airport and deposited them many hours later, hysterical and crying at the agency door, every one of them certain they had escaped Pol Pot only to die in Dallas traffic with a lunatic at the wheel.

A general consensus was very quickly made within the Cambodian community that I should be avoided. Tricia shifted my attention onto the asylum seekers from the Eastern Bloc. A newly arrived group of three was waiting to speak with her, but Tricia was running an hour late and asked if I would spend the time conversing with them. They had been learning English while in asylum camps in Europe, but she didn't feel they were very proficient. To give them a chance to practice, she suggested I go to the convenience store and buy a couple of sports magazines, as the men were all keen on soccer and sports in general, and then use the articles to initiate conversation.

In the long list of things I knew nothing about, sports and sports magazines were close to the top. Thinking myself clever, I scanned the periodicals and picked the ones with the word sports in the title. I came back with the October editions of *Sports Afield* and *American Sportsman*, unaware there was a difference between sports in an arena and sports in the woods.

For thirty minutes, I flipped through the pages, trying to initiate conversation, commenting, "And here's another double-barreled shotgun."

But the men would only stare at the carpet.

"Well, as none of you will say whether you've used one, there's not much for us to discuss there." Turning the page, I offered, "Let's see what else there is. Oh look, a bolt-action rifle. Any experience with one of these?"

The men had just come from the Soviet Bloc, and unbeknownst to me, their paranoia turned my ignorance into one of the most surreal interrogations they had ever endured. Experience told them they shouldn't cooperate, but Tricia had set me the task to get them speaking, so I kept trying.

After the pistols were emphatically denied, I read aloud, "Well, this says it's a M21 sniper rifle adapted from the M14," but then sounding rather dejected, "I already know none of you are going to admit to using that."

The weapons advertisements covered half the page, making the pictures impossible to overlook, but still Eugene and Daniel would scarcely glance at what I pointed to. They kept their faces blank, divulging nothing, and refused to interact, which left only Sergiu hiding a smirk behind his hand.

His enjoyment was not the only thing that set him apart. He didn't look like the other two either. There was something about the way Eastern Europeans dressed that marked them as foreign. It was the way they matched different prints and textured fabrics. Stripes might be paired with argyle, or a polka dot tie worn under a hideous snowflake sweater, and the socks would be business thin in running shoes. They seemed incapable of matching styles. But Sergiu was dressed in a dark suit with a plain shirt, and where the Romanians would have finished this look with Nike sneakers, Sergiu was wearing appropriately shined leather.

I didn't doubt that Sergiu was the one wearing Givenchy either. It was a heavy masculine scent, smelling rather like a leather boxing glove pounding on a patchouli-scented hippie. Violent yet spiritual.

Besides his cheerful mannerisms, his wardrobe, and cologne, there was another difference: he wasn't small or thin like his comrades, but was instead a big barrel of a man that overfilled the small seats in the agency's front room.

They were all about the same age, somewhere in their mid-thirties, but this and a common language were the only things they appeared to share.

Alarmed by my strange and inexplicable questioning of their experience with weapons, Eugene and Daniel stared at the floor, convinced I was a government agent, but Sergiu wasn't the slightest bit concerned. He kept his finger curled hard against his lips to keep from smiling, shaking his head no to each inquiry I made, but at the same time raising a brow as if in doubt I had actually asked, "Not one of you has fired a gun?"

I flipped the page and it was finally more than Sergiu could take. He saw something he recognized. His smile broke free and he leaned forward to point out, "AK-47. Eugene, Daniel, you know this, Kalashnikov AK-47."

But they both looked away making Sergiu laugh aloud.

The conversation dropped into stilted Romanian, full of terse warnings and suspicious glances that did not exactly fall on me but in my direction. Eugene took the offending magazine from my hands and started to absently fan through the glossy images, as though we could be done with it faster. At the back, he stopped on a block of type. He passed it to Daniel, and they studied it together, then returned it to me, asking, "What is this?"

I read it twice before explaining, "It's an ad for a mercenary." Then when all three men looked at me from the top of their eyes, I clarified, "Someone who accepts payment for fighting." And then even plainer, "For shooting people."

"This is job in America?"

"Well," I considered the ad again, "it appears so."

While Daniel and Eugene exchanged apprehensive glances, Sergiu gave up trying to conceal his humor.

"Constanzia?" he pointed at the ad and then to another magazine opened to a scoped rifle, "You like this?"

"I thought you did. It's sports."

"This is sports in America?" Eugene had been a professional tennis player and Daniel had been a professional soccer player, and both were hoping what I said wasn't true.

I was shrugging but not inclined to argue with the titles of the magazines when Sergiu started chuckling. "I think you play trick, Constanzia. I think you play trick on everyone. You make your face," he turned his features deadpan serious, "but you laughing. This very good trick," he smiled like we were sharing the joke, but then abruptly he ceased to show any humor. Leaning forward to bring his face close to mine, he was severe, "But you remember, you no trick me."

~~~~~~

When Tricia told me the twenty-odd men from the Eastern Bloc were afraid of me, I laughed.

She said, "I knew you would react like that. You don't see it, but you scare them."

"There is nothing even remotely frightening about me."

"Imagine it from their perspective. I cannot explain who you are or where you come from. And because you work here as a

57

volunteer, this makes them very suspicious. They don't understand why you would not work somewhere for pay."

"Because I do not have the thing you say I need."

"A green card. But they don't believe this, or how else would you be here with the agency?" Tricia grinned, "They think you are a government agent that has bamboozled me."

I laughed again.

"It is the way things work in their country."

It was comically absurd that anyone would think me tough or forceful enough to be either FBI or CIA, but apparently, "Your gentle mannerism is what makes you particularly dangerous."

It was funny to consider, but I didn't believe it. I tried to convince Tricia she had heard the men wrong, that the misunderstanding was one of language, but then after two weeks of thwarted efforts, I suspected she was right.

I would spend hours on the phone arranging job interviews for the Eastern Europeans, and the men would say to me, "Yes, yes, thank you, I go to interview," but then they wouldn't. I would call the prospective employer once more, apologizing, charming, lying, saying, "It was my fault, I gave the wrong date," or, "the wrong address." I'd reschedule and then implore the wary men not to make me look unreliable again, pressing them to accept my offer to drive them to the appointment, cornering them with solicitous attention, freaking them out until they assured me, "I go, I go." And they would go, making their own way there only to stare at the floor, mute with passive resistance, or outright decline the offer of employment.

Tricia would warn them, "There is only so long the agency can afford to support you. You need to accept the next offer." But if the job had been arranged by me, the suspected government agent, the offer was refused.

For camaraderie and support, all the Eastern Europeans had been settled into one apartment complex. In an attempt to make them more comfortable with me, Tricia started going to the complex to do paperwork and see how they were getting on, taking me with her to arrange for furniture and other essentials that would help transition them into the United States. Alone among the men was Sergiu who did not require the assistance of the agency to pay either his rent or the utilities, and not once did he ask for money to buy groceries. He shared a three-bedroom apartment with Eugene and Daniel, but they had no need for furnishings as Sergiu had decorated the place. Black leather couches and chrome tables sat on grungy brown carpet, and garishly framed oil paintings hung on the white, patched walls. The rundown apartment had never seen anything like it, and Sergiu, with his affable humor barely contained, sat amongst it in a beautifully stitched suit telling Tricia he had a job as a dishwasher.

"Excellent," Tricia commended him. "Where are you working?"

"Restaurant," he flicked it away.

"Yes, but which one?"

"Ah ..." he rolled his hands, one loosely circling the other, thinking, stretching out time. Taking a breath, he looked up to the mismatched spackled ceiling and frowned. Finally, he dismissed the question with an open palm, "I no remember name. But good place. Very nice."

"Do you think they could hire more, like Daniel and Eugene?"

Sergiu's eyes widened with his smile as he tried not to laugh. "Ah ... yes," flex of the shoulders and turn of the head. "Yes, maybe this okay."

"Will you ask?"

He'd already been chuckling under his breath, but when he saw Tricia was seriously waiting for a response, he threw his hands up and laughed loud, "Yes, I ask." Then, still laughing, he said to Eugene and Daniel, "Maybe we dishwasher together."

~~~~~

Tricia had a private matter to discuss with a Bulgarian in an apartment across the courtyard and told Sergiu, "If you don't mind, I will leave Constance here with you for the moment."

"Yes, yes, good," he fluffed the air in front of him, sending Tricia out the door. To me he said, "Constanzia, you make us coffee," gesturing in a circle around the room to include himself, Eugene, and Daniel.

Sure, okay. Perhaps I should have been insulted to be dismissed to the kitchen, but I had absolutely no opinion about it. I simply got up and went to investigate the coffee maker. It was a standard electric machine, but I had no idea how to use it. I examined it from top to bottom then started pulling and prying at the parts. Finding the swinging bowl that held the grounds, I searched through the cabinets to locate the beans. Five pounds of canned coffee in hand, I treated the electric maker like a stovetop percolator and dumped the grounds into the basket without a filter. Having nothing else to go by, it seemed reasonable to fill it to the top.

I was tap, tap, tapping the can on the edge of the plastic basket, scattering dark grounds across the chipped Formica counter, struggling to keep the wide brim from spilling its contents over the edge. The whole process was taking ages, but I was concentrating hard, determined to get it done.

I didn't know Sergiu was at my side until I smelled the heavy scent of Givenchy over the coffee. Holding the can still, I stopped to look at him and he asked painfully, "*Why*, Constanzia? I good with you. Why this," he indicated the coffee maker, "with me?"

I stared at him, baffled.

He glanced at the amount of grounds already in the basket. "You try hurt me? Maybe you think I no ..." he punched his chest.

My furrowed brow meant I was clueless as to what he meant. I studied both him and the coffee maker for meaning.

"This how you make coffee?" he demanded.

I set the can down. "I thought so, but I've never made it before."

His head dropped forward to consider me with disbelief. Raising his brows, he stared at me, waiting for me to change my story or give something more, and when I did neither, he pulled back with a deep breath to ask gravely, "You laughing at me?"

I looked myself over and then, rather perplexed it wasn't obvious, answered, "No."

He exhaled confusion. At a loss to understand, he put both his hands on my shoulders and stepped me to the side to stand before the coffee maker himself.

Palms open to encompass the mess I had made, he shook his head muttering, "Madonna mia."

Pulling the basket out of the machine and dumping the grounds in the trash, he spoke aloud as though he were explaining it to us both, "So, you no laughing whole time." Rinsing the basket, stating as fact, "You think Kalashnikov is sport." Showing me the filters and then daintily taking one to press into the basket, he held it for me to inspect. "You know how to cook?"

I looked around the kitchen as though it were a hospital operating theater.

He asked himself sardonically, "Why she know how to cook when she make coffee like this?" He swept his hand over the counter, pushing a pile of grounds to one side. "How many years you have?" He was filling the jug with water, waiting for my answer, but I was confused. He searched for the phrase he'd been taught, "How old are you?"

"Twenty-three."

He laughed. Pointing at the two and then just below the four cup measuring lines, he asked, "Two three?"

"Yes."

"No." Pouring the water into the coffee maker, "Why you say this, Constanzia?" But I remained silent while he scooped an appropriate amount of grounds into the filter. Once the machine was started, he watched it like he were in a daze, then huffing out a breath, he turned to look me over and declare, "Maybe you one nine. *Maybe*."

I smiled an expression of whatever-makes-you-happy, making Sergiu frown and say, "You pretty girl but," his hand waved from the left of me to the right, "something no good with you." Then, after a moment's consideration, "I like this."

CAMBODIAN MOB

Sitting on Tricia's front porch, we were looking over the park. Tricia was worried. She didn't want to sound paranoid, but she wondered if maybe someone were watching the house.

I shielded my eyes to squint into the setting sun. In the farthest distance, golfers were striking balls across the green, but no one else seemed to be around.

"Perhaps I'll ask your detective what he thinks when he gets here."

We were waiting for Rick to arrive. He'd called from the sheriff's office while I was working. I'd been with Tricia for a month and he'd been meaning to check up on me, so he offered, "We'll make a night of it, and I'll take you to dinner."

But first Tricia wanted to tell me something. She'd been edgy the past week. We would go to see the Europeans and she'd keep her attention out the window, looking, watching. Sergiu would press wine on her, but she was too agitated to drink it.

He had asked me, "What is problem with Tricia?"

But I didn't know. I hadn't asked. She always seemed relatively calm in his living room with Daniel. It was with the Cambodians she was really troubled.

And tonight it seemed like we were at the Asian apartment complex instead of her porch. She was jumpy, looking nearly manic while throwing back wine to drown her nerves. Her asking Rick if someone was watching the house sounded positively demented, and I was embarrassed for us both just imagining it. Hoping to prevent any such wild speculations from being voiced, I was keeping a lookout for Rick's black SUV.

Tricia had just started explaining, "There's something going on at the agency," when a new Porsche Carrera stopped in front of the house. Sergiu and Daniel got out, but their arrival made no difference. Tricia was primed by two glasses of wine to share her concerns.

She was so obviously disturbed that the men approached quizzically, their faces showing instant compassion, both of them ready to assist or avenge. The whole Eastern Bloc of refugees adored Tricia.

She had given Daniel the address, but they weren't expected, and the reason for their visit wasn't questioned with Tricia's distress.

Pulling a seat close to her side, Daniel patted her arm and asked, "What? What is it?"

And Sergiu stood with one foot on the steps, rolling his hand to encourage her to speak.

She spoke to no one in particular, "I have file after file of missing Cambodian women, and not a soul can tell me where they've gone. They arrived at the airport and then, *poof*, disappeared."

Sergui, Daniel, and I took a moment to shift back for a little distance and perspective. We all turned our heads as though we might hear it better in an echo. We were waiting for more, but Tricia was silent.

I had to speak for us all, suggesting, "You might want to explain that a little further."

She'd taken over as director of the refugee agency some six months previous and noticed there was a large influx of young, single Cambodian women being sponsored by various churches and families in Dallas, but, upon arrival in the United States, they never made contact with the agency. In the past few weeks, she had started to track them down, but every time she called the pastors or families to inquire if the women required any support or assistance, she heard the same story: "We've never seen her."

"You signed the sponsorship papers," Tricia accused them, "and you've made no attempt to meet her?"

In every case, the sponsor couldn't tell Tricia where the woman was because a Cambodian relative, either her brother or uncle, had insisted on picking her up from the airport. "She's gone to live with her family," they told Tricia. "We weren't concerned because it's what we expected from the start."

When the uncle had come asking for sponsorship, he'd made assurances it was merely paperwork and the woman would require no further assistance. The sponsors thought they had been acting charitably, getting the woman out of an asylum camp, certain she had family in Dallas waiting on her.

But the agency's books listed no relatives. Tricia started searching the years before she had arrived and found countless more instances of women vanishing at the airport.

She looked at me and said, "I thought this was the sort of thing you might know something about."

Neither Sergiu nor Daniel knew my story, so Sergiu was bewildered. "Why Constanzia know anything about this?"

66

I was still oblivious to what I had implied about myself, and Tricia wasn't going to reveal what everyone else thought of me. She gestured for me to clarify and looked away.

Truly perplexed, I shrugged my shoulders and Sergiu didn't doubt I was sincere. He cut his hand straight through the misunderstanding, his expression reading, "Never mind, it's the stress."

Shaking the notion out of his thoughts, he explained to Tricia, "This is problem you have with mob. Cambodian mob. Is problem." He'd been nodding his head, calmly reinforcing Tricia's suspicions before casually adding, "They have many prostitutes."

"Yes," Tricia pointed at him like he was the backup she'd been looking for, "that was my exact fear."

"The Cambogianis give straw to the fire," Sergiu seemed to be taking it personally. "Maybe problem terminate soon."

Tricia scowled her confusion at him. The Cambodian mob was going nowhere. They were one of the top stories in the newspaper. In less than a decade, they'd displaced the Italian and Mexican criminal gangs in Dallas, and no one knew what to do with them because they hacked people to death for minor offenses. When angered, they were known for being especially grisly. The Cambodians had seen way too much under Pol Pot's rule to think a baseball bat to the knees was anything more than a friendly tickle in a territorial dispute.

The refugee agency took in significantly more Cambodians than Eastern Europeans but spent a quarter of the time on them, only helping in the first weeks of their arrival, because after that the mob would have made contact, and they alone dispensed assistance. Any support provided outside their influence made them look bad, and everyone quickly learned you didn't want to make the Cambodian mob look bad.

And anyway, Tricia would later ask me, "What could Sergiu possibly know of it having just come from Romania?"

I thought very little of any of it. All of this was just background noise while I waited for Rick and Interpol and the FBI to figure out who I was. In my wildest flights of fancy, I hoped I might fit the description of a child abducted in Europe and her family might claim me as their own. That would be exciting. I'd get to go to Europe. But even if nothing like that ever happened, at some point the authorities would give me legitimate identification, and then my real life in Dallas would begin. Until then, I was just passing meaningless time.

The last thing I wanted was for the drama playing out on the porch to spill over into my future, and around the corner I had seen Rick's SUV turn onto our street. I rose and said, "We should take this inside. Come gentlemen, we've been very rude. We should have offered you something to drink."

Then once I had everyone over the threshold, I pulled back saying, "I'll join you after I get the mail," but instead, I shut the door and left with Rick.

~~~~~~

The detective in Rick had taken note of the shiny Porsche sitting outside Tricia's middle-class bungalow. It meant very little to me, and when pressed to think about it, I assumed there was a perfectly reasonable explanation for why two new immigrants to the United States were in possession of it.

Rick tried to discuss it casually, saying, "It appears to be new."

But his suspicion was apparent, so I only answered, "Oh," as though I were disinterested to hear it.

"It's a very expensive car."

"Hmm," my interest was no more engaged.

"You'd have to be quite wealthy to afford one."

"Mmm."

"Is it Tricia's?"

"No."

Rick had already had too many of these conversations not to realize it would go nowhere without a direct question. "Do you know who owns it?"

"No."

"It's just parked outside Tricia's house?"

"Yes." All technically true. Not that I'd had a sudden crisis of conscience and thought I should be honest with Rick, but over the matter of the car, I had no reason to outright lie to him either, yet his presumption that something was amiss made me cautious.

I shifted the topic, saying, "It's nice to see you again," forcing Rick to move along or be openly distrustful.

And he did consider it, but then he set the subject aside. There were more relevant matters to discuss. He had a stack of forms from

Interpol, and he didn't have the answers to most of the questions. Neither did I.

Date of birth was unknown, as was living family members, and I couldn't say exactly where I had lived the last five years. Place of birth was probably Europe. The doctors at the psychiatric hospital had already determined I was not born in the United States because I did not have the immunization scar most adults had on their arm. I'd gotten lucky there. My childhood doctor had thought such blemishes were ugly and had hid it on my thigh.

When Rick asked if I spoke another language, I thought it might be beneficial to instill a bit of doubt, so I let the question sit for a while before answering, "No."

"Are you sure?"

A little more uncertainty and then, "Yes."

"Yes to a second language?"

I gave an expression that I might admit it, almost said what it was but changed my mind, "No." I decided then that I needed to learn Russian. With the Cold War at its height, that would be sinister.

Under language, Rick wrote that I spoke English with a British accent.

Education was private tutors. My appearance was well-presented, and my manner polished and refined.

I had no tattoos, but there was an obvious scar on my cheek and another above it on my brow. "I was a clumsy child," there was no reason to lie about that. I had been four and remembered both times I split my face open falling into a table, but I didn't want to tell a story about an emergency room visit, so regarding the details, I insisted, "I don't remember."

Rick was quiet. He was thinking, and whatever he was thinking about did not make him happy. Finally he asked, "Did someone hit you?"

"*No*," with two syllables. I was baffled as to who he thought would dare to strike me. I was a countess. Countesses did not get hit. But I could see he didn't believe me, so I said with greater insistence, "No."

The section of the form we were discussing dealt with identifying body marks, and he was looking at the scar forming on my wrist. He decided to fill that part in later and flipped the page, and then maybe he would fill in the next few pages about my background without me present as well.

He would attach my fingerprints and photograph later.

But as long as he was asking, he had just one more question about the Porsche, "When did it show up?"

And as long as I was lying, "I have no idea."

~~~~~~

Tricia was compiling a list of Cambodian women that the refugee agency had never made contact with and who she could learn nothing about. Their folders were grouped together in the top drawer of her office filing cabinet. To prevent losing any more, I went to the airport to meet the next single woman due to arrive.

I was at the arrival gate looking for a solitary Cambodian woman, and was the first to approach her, asking her name, "Chantou?"

And that was the extent of my Khmer. I knew nothing else in the language.

When she agreed this was her name, I smiled to indicate I was friendly and motioned she should come with me. Then, a middle-aged Cambodian man joined us and asked of her considerably more. We walked together toward baggage claim with the man conversing, and Chantou agreeing. I could offer nothing.

At the turnstile, Chantou pointed to a box wrapped in black plastic. The man and I both tried to claim possession of it, but he was faster. I went to pull it from his arms and he resisted, swinging the box away. Understanding Chantou would follow the box, I took hold of his arm, saying, "You have no business here, now give that to me."

And he had quite a lot to say in Khmer, which alarmed Chantou.

Hands out to pacify, I was explaining as though Chantou might understand, "It's okay, I'm with the refugee agency. You really do want to come with me."

But I imagine she was hearing from the man, "The crazy white woman plans to slaughter and eat you," because she went full-tilt rollercoaster screaming.

It was loud.

I stepped back, and then back again. Hands up to surrender any claim on the box, I was pleading, "Oh please, please don't do that. It's okay," but no one around us thought so.

There were few things worse to me than a scene, and Chantou had us center stage at the baggage claim. I wanted to flee but Tricia had told me a terrible story about what would become of Chantou if the Cambodian mob left the airport with her.

Sergiu had explained it in detail to Tricia, telling her that first Chantou would have her passport taken away, and then be told she was indebted to the mob for expenses incurred getting her out of the asylum camp. Chantou would either be isolated or imprisoned with other girls in the same situation, but she'd have no opportunity to make contact with outside help or reveal her circumstances to anyone.

If she were a European, Sergiu explained, she would probably have to be smacked around or beaten into compliance, but he doubted after all that had occurred under the Khmer Rouge the woman would have much fight left.

To pay off her debt, Chantou would be required to work for the mob. She would never know how much her body was being sold for, and the debt she owed to the mob would increase as they fed, clothed, and housed her. In the decade it took her to clear the balance, she would likely become a willing participant, even manipulating other young women who arrived to find themselves in the same position. And then, when she was too old to sell, if she hadn't first killed herself, been murdered, or overdosed, she'd likely become a house matron, or madame.

And no amount of language charades would allow me to convey this to her.

The man at her side spoke Khmer, and he was telling her something truly terrifying about me, shoving her forward with the box, prodding her toward the exit.

I was following, imploring, "Please, Chantou, please just wait."

But she was backing away, pointing at me with wild accusations that fell into loud heaving sobs.

Then security arrived.

I learned the Cambodian spoke English. He said, "This woman is assaulting my niece."

And Chantou wailed agreement.

The guard stopped me while they scurried fast steps for the sliding doors. I tried to explain, "I'm with the Dallas Fort Worth Refugee Agency, and I've been sent to collect that woman. She's an asylum seeker."

"She seems to be happy with everything except you," the guard said. "Do you have a badge or ID?"

"Not on me, but if you'll give me a moment, I will get it." I watched Chantou merge into the crowd outside the airport and said, "It's with my associate in the car. I'll just go get it." But there was no one in the car and I was driving without a license.

The guard held my arm and suggested, "How about you wait with me for a second?"

"How about not?"

I'd taken us both forward but he hauled us back, proposing, "How about you come with me then?" and walked us through the curious observers. But it was nothing more than a stroll through the turnstiles, wasting time until Chantou and her uncle could leave the area. Off at the empty edge of baggage claim, he released my arm with another suggestion, "Now, how about you go home?"

~~~~~~

It was agreed, I was not the best person to collect women from the airport. Tricia needed to go with someone who spoke Khmer, but no one capable in the language was willing to step into mob territory.

She spoke with an officer who acted as one of the liaisons between the police force and the Cambodian community. He wasn't surprised to hear anything Tricia said, but he thought there were a few things she should know. Chief among them, the Cambodians were tight and they didn't talk, especially not to the police who they didn't trust. And in case she hadn't heard, the mob was ruthless. The officer had seen a hatchet job of theirs that had required all the carpets to be replaced, both in the apartment on the third floor where the incident had taken place and also in the apartment under it on the second floor.

What Tricia was saying about the missing women was sad, he granted, but an investigation would go nowhere as no one would talk. About all he suspected would come of probing it would be her death. If that's how she wanted to open the investigation, "Well, that will be the open and close of it, because the Cambodians still won't talk."

While Tricia was mulling over that brush off, Mike made a visit to the refugee agency to see how I was getting along. Being as he was ex-FBI, Tricia explained to him about the missing women. He heard it all out, asked some questions, and then wanted to know why she was telling him and not the police.

"Could I take this to the FBI?"

He knew what she hoped to hear and frowned to have to tell her, "I doubt it would be a large enough case to interest the FBI. What you are describing is a matter for the police."

But before Tricia approached the police again, she wanted more evidence. She wanted to drop undeniable proof on their desks. She understood the Cambodians weren't going to talk, but there was still the possibility that an American might know something.

HORSE POWER

Sergiu thought he was punishing me by not speaking to me in the weeks after I left surreptitiously with Rick, but I hadn't noticed, so Daniel was forced to explain it to me. "He was very hurt and angry."

"*Why?*"

"I think you know."

But I didn't. And I didn't care enough to press. The whole Eastern Bloc of men were an unending frustration to me, never going for the job interviews I arranged, or sabotaging the ones they did. Eugene and Daniel still hadn't accepted employment even though I had all but guaranteed them a dozen opportunities.

Daniel had arrived at Tricia's house in a new BMW to tell me Sergiu had forgiven me and was coming to take me to dinner. Daniel had come with a bag of groceries and a plan to cook moussaka for Tricia, and he wanted me out of the house.

And I did what I was told. Get in the car. *Sure*. Make coffee. *Of course*. Pick people up at the airport. *You got it*. Go eat dinner with Sergiu. *Okay*.

I never said no.

Tricia thought it was my submissive training, years spent acquiescing to a master, but it was my adolescent mentality. I was out of my league, frequently overwhelmed by some new experience but on constant guard not to reveal surprise, thinking everything — the dismembered Cambodians, the missing women, Sergiu's parade of expensive cars — was all just part of the adult world I had staked claim to. I was deeply tired trying to understand it, and every other bit of minutia as well, all the while maintaining pretenses, careful not to let my English accent slip or expose myself as a fraud. Having done one giant fuck-you-rebellion in getting to Dallas, my beleaguered mind was content to follow directions.

When Sergiu arrived, he said, "Constanzia, come," and held out his arm to take possession of me. I was already familiar with this habit of his. Countless times before he'd had his hand on my shoulder, guiding me as though I might get lost crossing the carpet. Few people around him were competent enough to transverse small distances without help. But he was rougher with the men. Daniel and Eugene would get shaken while he laughed, gripped until they winced, or pulled into a good-natured, bone-rattling side-hug.

Within the first week of meeting Sergiu, I'd already given up trying to walk unassisted. At first I had tried to drop away, slinking off to the side to slip his hold, but this tended to result in a series of correcting dance steps, or worse, the question, "Why you act like this? I good with you. You want hurt me?" He'd touch his heart, and I'd feel guilty.

Thinking I had made an appalling social plunder, I'd apologize and he'd consider my sincerity. Then he'd smile, pat me on the cheek, and carry on directing me across the floor.

It was preferable to how he handled others. A newly arrived Bulgarian had tried to shirk him and Sergiu had seized onto his shoulder until the man was bending with the pain, but Sergiu was slapping him in the stomach, laughing, jostling him until the

Bulgarian returned forced amusement, agreeing to whatever Sergiu said.

I figured it was cultural and was glad Sergiu was gentle with me. He was directing our path to the black Corvette three houses away, asking, "You understand Spanish?"

"No."

"Is no problem." He took us to a Mexican restaurant where he spoke easily with the staff, ordering for us both, before returning to fractured English to converse with me.

Three hours later he pulled back from our conversation to look me over with surprise. "This is first time I see you like this. You very …" he went looking for the word he knew in four languages but I didn't understand any of them. He asked the server for the word in English and the server asked another and pretty soon every employee was looking for the English equivalent of a Spanish compliment.

No one knew it. But the table behind us had started bickering. It escalated until the Texan slammed down his beer, plunked on his cowboy hat, and stalked out the door. The Mexican woman was finally free to talk and came around to speak to me. "You are very charming. This is what the gentleman wants to say."

And the staff confirmed, "Sí, sí, es charming," offering again to Sergiu, "charming."

But he wasn't listening, instead we were both watching the woman from the adjoining table. She had the first hint of gray in her hair, but it looked premature. She wasn't happy. She was leaving but needed to explain, "I never wanted to be the couple that sat silent in a restaurant with nothing to say. It was a mistake learning English. We had more to say when we couldn't say it."

~~~~~

It was just before midnight when Sergiu and I returned to the house. Daniel was working hard to seduce Tricia, so, to give him space, Sergiu offered to let me drive the sports car.

Now this was a real mistake.

No one in Texas had seen how quickly my personality could flip. Sergiu now knew I could be charming, but he assumed this was merely an extension of my demure character. He didn't know I liked to charge horses. I'd race them, mad to frothing, into goats, people, and tobacco fields, and then laugh when scolded. I loved the rush and my favorite horse wanted to be let loose without reigns.

Nothing about my reserved demeanor had prepared Sergiu for what was about to happen.

But the moment I popped the Corvette into first gear, I was certain the engine was screaming to be unbridled, and I was manic to set it free.

The car could charge, and I was racing around the narrow neighborhood streets trying to reach eighty with Sergiu shouting, "Stop! Constanzia, stop! This is not my car. My friends be very mad if you hurt it."

And the car already seemed to be in pain. I'd never driven a manual but I'd watched Sergiu and the process looked simple. He made it seem like a fluid exchange of gas and clutch, but my attempts to emulate him just ground against the gears. I handled it by going faster, revving the RPMs into red and then lunging the car forward so both Sergiu and I were slammed back.

Thinking to halt the insanity, he grabbed my right wrist as I shifted down to second, squealing into a turn, but I accelerated regardless, taking my other hand off the wheel to lurch the car into third. Pressing hard on the gas, and about to use my left hand again for fourth, he released my right hoping I'd keep control, but it scarcely made a difference; I kept us on the edge of wrecking.

The nose was too long and, unlike a horse, it couldn't direct itself. Twice I nearly put the headlights into a parked car while skidding around a corner, Sergiu exclaiming, "*Oddio!*"

Then I shot us across a dark lawn, bottoming out with horrific noise on the curb, while he shrieked, "*Madonna mia!*"

And in between it all was a string of language I only partially understood, but I knew he was calling me crazy, was swearing and begging, threatening and bargaining, never realizing there was nothing he could offer that could compare to the power under my foot. It was truly the most fun I had ever had.

He wanted to take the wheel from my hands but didn't dare at the speeds I was reaching, and the interior of the car was too tight for him to get his foot across the gearbox and onto the brake. With one hand on the back of my neck, wanting to wring it, and the other braced against the dash, he could only bellow and then plead with me for restraint.

About ten minutes into the ride of terror, I stalled the Corvette trying to do donuts on the golf course green.

I was reaching for the ignition key again, finally seeing there wasn't one, and then Sergiu got my wrists. Hauled straight over the transmission, we were both going out the passenger door.

I didn't comprehend but three foreign words of what he was roaring, but I understood the tone. Holding me against the car with one hand, he'd thrown his other open to encompass the circles of torn up grass, and I imagined he was cursing, "A golf course, for Christ's sake!" and next he was shaking me, saying something about the police.

Then, one hand around my neck, he was threatening with the other to slap me, but I wasn't paying attention. I was consumed by something else. Leaning into him to breathe deep, he was just like a horse whose scent had been raised with its blood. I said, "You always smell like Givenchy."

Taken aback, he hit the roof of the car instead.

Then, with his finger in my face, the tirade continued but I hadn't even flinched; I was still drawing in the fragrance as he demanded, something-something "you crazy?"

I replied with unaffected serenity, "The asylum said no."

Sergiu stalked away only to turn and bound back, slamming both hands on the top of the car's frame, pinning me to the door, expecting something more than my continued interest in his cologne, but when all he got was me pressing my face into his jacket to inhale, he heaved frustration from his lungs and opened the passenger door to push me in.

While he crossed behind the car, I saw the ignition key on the floor and reached to collect it. It had been filed down to a thin line, no grooves whatsoever, no grip to hold it in place on a wild ride, but most importantly, it should not have turned over the engine.

I handed it to Sergiu with a smirk.

The whole ride back was a long incomprehensible rant that he gave to himself in what sounded like four different languages, and only briefly was one of them English. "This girl is no good. No good. No *bueno*, no *buona*, no *bun*. No more with this girl."

~~~~~~~

Daniel was on the porch with Tricia waiting for Sergiu, and at the curb, Eugene was adjusting the radio dial in a Saab. All three were driving that night to New York and planned to fly back later in the week. Daniel had said they were working for a wealthy businessman, conveying cars bought at auction to a dealership. And while he confided it was too good of money to pass up, he considered the job strictly temporary until he found something else.

"Constance, you come to airport for us?" Tricia had already volunteered me in the agency's car, but Daniel wanted it confirmed.

But on hearing it, Sergiu erupted in Romanian. Pacing between the curb and the porch, he directed Daniel's attention to the mud sprayed across the back fenders and then pointed at the golf course, all the while raging loud and throwing his arms wide to emphasize the insolence he'd endured.

I shrugged my shoulders at Tricia as though the scene playing out across the lawn was utterly inexplicable.

The close tussle against the car had left me smelling like him, and the scent almost made me want to apologize. I even turned before retiring into the house, had the words "I'm sorry" in my mouth, but he was still seething and I thought it would probably be easier to just go buy a bottle of Givenchy.

It took all of the days he was away for Sergiu to find anything remotely humorous about that night. He returned with annoyance still pinching at his eyes, informing me we were going to dinner. Once in the Jaguar, he tried to explain his frustration. "You always calm. You," his hand dropped across his face to erase all but the merest hint of a smile, and he spoke with a near comatose expression, "You show nothing. You say, 'Yes, Sergiu,' and, 'Of course, Sergiu,' but nothing here," he punched his heart. "But you sit here," indicating the driver's seat, "and ahi," hands up and screaming followed by "brum," his arm shot off down the road. He barely managed to chuckle, "You no drive again."

I'd already seen the Jaguar key with no teeth turn the ignition and thought his assertion was highly unlikely, but I wasn't going to give him any cause to suspect it. I nodded and looked out the window, mostly just glad to be out of the house. Tricia was having nightly asthma attacks brought on by stress. She knew the cause of it, but she wouldn't stop searching for the missing women.

The agency was overseen by a board of directors and Jeff was Tricia's primary contact among them. I had listened to Tricia's even voice behind the partitions at work as she quietly told Jeff her concerns. She'd flipped through the growing stack of files, counting off the young women who had arrived at the Dallas/Fort Worth Airport only to vanish.

Jeff's tone was at first soothing, sounding like he was placating, whispering something smooth like, *No, no, you've got it all wrong. Everything is fine.*

Tricia tried to make him understand. "No communication has ever been established. The women have no known addresses. And no one will admit to meeting them."

Jeff kept giving soft assurances, sounding like a father putting a troubled child to sleep, murmuring things I could only imagine. *Hush now, nothing lives under the bed.*

But Tricia was clear and insistent, "I can't find the most recent woman, Chantou. No one's heard of her."

It's the dark, shhh, you're imagining things.

"Who was the man? No one will say."

There are no monsters in the closet.

"But he took her and she's gone."

And no faces in the window either.

Then, Tricia mentioned the Cambodian mob.

Now Jeff was grumbling angrily. A filing drawer in her office slammed shut. Something else, a coffee cup or fist, came down hard on her desk, and finally Tricia was silenced.

Jeff stamped out through the lobby and hit the front door with his open palm. He'd thrown it wide to slam against the weatherboards and wasn't stopping to close it.

I went around the corner to find Tricia ashen, too stunned for asthma, asking, "Did you hear that?"

"Most of it."

"Does he know?"

"It does appear that way."

She spent the next week trying to find the former director of the refugee agency, wanting to know what he knew and why he left. There was no clue of who he'd been in any of the agency's books, so she went covertly to another member of the board for the information.

"It was something Jacobs," but the board member couldn't remember and would have to get back to Tricia. Then unwittingly, the matter was referred to Jeff to deal with.

Jeff was on the phone shouting loud enough through Tricia's earpiece for me to hear at my desk.

Through it all, I'd been a teenager, oblivious to danger, unconcerned with mortality, thinking if there was any reason to be alarmed someone would surely react. As far as I knew, everything that was occurring was perfectly common.

Tricia was on edge, and she was having asthma attacks, but she wasn't running or screaming. When she looked to me for support to continue, I'd glance up from my book and think it made perfect sense to carry on with the plot.

"Turn the page. Let's see what happens," was my advice.

And I held what she was doing as secret as I did everything else. I didn't mention the events at the refugee agency to Rick or Sergiu or anyone. Dinner with Rick had nothing to do with dinner with Sergiu, and life with Tricia was private. If she wanted to chase the Cambodian mob and missing women, I'd no more speak of it than mention Sergiu and Daniel's weekly trips to New York.

FALSE GODS

It was November and I had been in Dallas for two months when I made the pilgrimage to Neiman Marcus. The documentary that had excited my young mind with inconceivable wealth had reiterated that Neiman Marcus could acquire absolutely anything you desired. You want a three tent circus? They could get it. You want two matching 20 carat black opals? Neiman Marcus would find them. Mink coats and diamonds were trivial to Neiman Marcus.

When I got identification and could finally start my life as a countess, this was the place I hoped to shop. The store was in the heart of downtown, and I entered the busy first floor with a crowd. There was not much to see. There was a café in the corner but little else to explain the bustle. I watched a mother and daughter ride the escalator to the upper levels and assumed the fur coats and stunning wardrobes lie above.

But the second floor was no larger than 20x20 feet wide, and it was empty. The walls and floor were beautifully colored, but they were bare. There was nothing: no pictures, no rugs, no racks, or shelves, or display cases. The place was barren. A solitary person by a featureless door considered me, and after a moment, deemed me just barely worthy, but before they could speak, I slipped around to continue up the escalator.

The third floor was the same but a different colour.

On the fourth floor, a stack of wool rugs were laid flat on the floor and the escalator ride was over.

Whatever the rich came to Neiman Marcus to buy, it wasn't made visible to the plebs. There was no sign of the mother and daughter. They had been welcomed through one of the doors into the private galleries.

Returning to the first floor, I watched the escalator.

I was vividly out of place. I did not look in any way similar to the people who ascended. The girls my age, my genuine age, in their teens, had wide ribbon bows in their hair. Every last one of them. I'd have to be held down and threatened with something greater than mortal embarrassment to wear a bow. It was the 80s when everyone had a perm, but I didn't need one. My hair was naturally curly. I loved my hair, but the women on the escalator had spurned the look. They had straight hair, bobbed at the shoulders and flicked up hard at the ends. Their hair was precise. I took scissors to my own with no concern about making it straight because anything uneven would just spring up into the coils and be lost. The Neiman Marcus clients looked sharp, and I appeared to have just stumbled in from the wind swept moors.

I wasn't wearing nearly enough cosmetics, or perfume, or jewels to pass as their kin. My clothes had been donated to the refugee agency, and while most of them bore designer labels, they lacked the brand-new-worn-only-once sheen of the truly wealthy. I watched them disappearing into Neiman Marcus's upper levels and knew they would spot me as a fraud.

~~~~~~

I never wanted to return to Neiman Marcus. It was disheartening. I didn't belong and I was fairly certain I would never be able to attain the severe appearance required of its women. It was better with Sergiu. He wore beautifully stitched suits with Italian labels. His watch was Bvlgari, his cologne Givenchy. He drove expensive cars and was as comfortable eating in a dark dive as any one of Dallas's finer restaurants.

He'd come to the house and say, "Constanzia, come," and I'd stop what I was doing to put on lipstick and shoes.

Wherever we went, we were accepted. And because we were foreign, I could have as crazy of hair as I liked.

But we didn't valet park. And the doors were left unlocked. Sergiu wore driving gloves and I essentially didn't touch anything, but none of this was mentioned.

Whether it was an Audi, Mercedes, or Porsche, he always had the appropriate emblem on the filed down key. It looked legitimate driving, but he didn't explain.

He was boisterous of voice but discreet with cash. We talked when others didn't, often drawing in the surrounding tables. After the woman's confession at the Mexican restaurant, Sergiu couldn't bear to see a quiet couple. Wherever we went, we would stay for hours and he could afford to give the miserable twenty minutes.

He was careful to work on the man. "This is very good drink. It makes me happy. You no so happy, I can see." And he'd order the uncommunicative fellow a duplicate. "You have beautiful wife –

pardon me for noticing. You are in beautiful place with beautiful food. But you have bad day, no?"

Sergiu would have the woman smiling and the man agreeing, as though it were in no way normal for them not to be speaking. It was all just a bad day.

"You drink and you forget. Constanzia tells me your wife maybe like this drink she like." The look between men was that neither of them would have it, but Sergiu would encourage, and the man would order his wife whatever cocktail Sergiu had ordered me.

One would always ask, "Where are you from?"

And depending on his mood, Sergiu might say Romania, Portugal, Spain, or Italy, but he'd twist it around to someplace the couple had traveled. He was brilliant. He'd make them laugh and then speak well of each other. And when he removed himself from their conversation, they were under pressure not to fall silent. People were watching.

~~~~~~

It was late when I got home from dinner with Sergiu. Tricia was still up and at the basin washing her face. I was watching her from the hall, leaning against the door frame, babbling something inconsequential when she rose up to the mirror. There were distinct finger marks bruising her throat.

"Tricia? What happened?"

"I've had a bad night," was her understatement.

90

She'd had a horrific encounter with Jeff preacher.

Jeff felt there was a misunderstanding bet suggested they resolve it at his office. He'd asked the large Cambodian church to attend, telling Tricia the man would be present to mediate. But the pair's insistence that she had her facts wrong was menacing, and only minutes into the meeting, Tricia felt threatened. She had watched me leave work with Sergiu and realized no one knew where she was.

When she tried to leave, the preacher blocked the door. Both he and Jeff wanted to hear assurances that she understood no women were missing. She wanted to agree but first she needed to dig in her purse for her inhaler.

Thinking she was reaching for a gun, the preacher splayed himself across the door screaming, and Jeff snatched her bag to search it while Tricia wheezed out the explanation, "Asthma."

Fifteen minutes later, she was swearing the issue had been resolved, harmony restored, and if they would only stand aside, she'd cease to be a problem.

Outside Jeff's office, the street was bright but the only way to her car was through an unlit alley. She didn't want to enter, but she didn't want to encounter Jeff again either, so she reasoned with herself, telling herself there was nothing to worry about, convincing herself the worst of the night was over. Halfway down the darkened lane, the very thing she feared stepped out of a black alcove. The same height as her, the Cambodian rammed her against the wall and then held her by the throat. She expected to be stabbed and hacked to

...rt as a gruesome warning to others who dared to question, the man barely moved. And he had nothing to say either. He just gripped her by the neck, rattling her small frame against the bricks to keep her attention, and stared silently in her eyes. Then unknown minutes later, as a second asthma attack choked her for breath, he released her. She backed away for the parking lot and he stood eerily at ease watching her go.

MAKING HEADLINES

At the end of November, Tricia resigned from the agency. Nothing had been resolved and Chantou hadn't been found. But we didn't talk about this. Any mention of the refugee agency would have Tricia wheezing for breath, suffering such debilitating asthma attacks, her inhaler was little help. She was being suffocated by guilt and fear; and though I didn't recognize it at the time, I do now, she was having panic attacks.

She seldom left the house anymore, so we spent our days at home. Daniel began spending more nights, paying for rent and groceries, and Sergiu came more frequently too. When they weren't driving to New York, he and Daniel would take over the kitchen and cook for hours. Sergiu was always trying to draw me into their spirited task, wanting to teach me something, like how to use a knife so every attempt didn't end with my blood staining the cutting board.

I'd pick up the knife and he'd cross himself, say a prayer to heaven, and then hover over me insisting, "The garlic no fight. Is nice garlic. You no try to kill." But he couldn't bear to watch and was too afraid to turn his back.

After the second mishap requiring liquid sutures, he wouldn't let me near anything sharp. Instead, he tried to show me how to core a head of lettuce by striking it once "at the base of skull, no, of root, this here."

"The stalk," I offered and noticed the punch exploded through the head to splay the leaves out like a bowl.

"Now it is cooperative."

He was boisterous and gregarious, dominating the scene, pulling everyone in, always animated and holding a laugh just beneath the surface. And he was passionate about dinner. It was the high point of every day. He complained that he could not fully express himself in English and if only I knew another language: Romanian, Italian, Spanish, Portuguese, even French would be better. "How you only know English?"

But even so, we never spent less than two hours at the table.

It was very different than eating with Rick.

Sergiu and Daniel had been in New York when Rick called. There was something we needed to discuss.

We were in a chain restaurant, and I was following Rick's subdued lead. The meal was one of good Southern manners, full of restraint and general pleasantries. At the end, he explained that my case was public record and had "gone out on the wire." Straight through October and now most of November, the Associated Press and a number of other reporters had harassed him to reveal my location. He had steadfastly refused, putting them off and making excuses to protect me, but he couldn't very well tell them he didn't know where I was, as, "That would make my office look unprofessional."

He didn't seem comfortable with the idea, and he was happy to keep turning them away, but if I wanted to speak with a reporter, there was a journalist from Austin whose inquiries were far more polite than the others.

I didn't know what to think of it. It sounded like I'd be putting myself forward for further scrutiny without benefit, but it also appealed to me as potentially diverting. I was torn, so I was ambiguous, responding with nothing more than an acknowledging smile.

Rick asked, "So, you'll speak with her?"

I raised my eyes in a wordless expression of *Should I?*

"Do you want to talk with her?"

I didn't know, so I wasn't helping. I'd found silence to be the best tactic when in doubt so far.

And when Rick finally recognized I wasn't giving any more, he said, "I'll give the journalist Tricia's phone number and you can think about it."

~~~~~~

Tricia couldn't think of a reason why I wouldn't talk to Patrice. It sounded quite exciting. Patrice was from the *Austin American Statesman* and she'd already spent an hour on the phone with Tricia privately discussing my story, asking Tricia what she could expect from me, how to approach, no doubt discussing the sensitive topic of my life as a submissive prostitute.

She came at the start of December while Sergiu and Daniel were away.

It had been over two months since anyone had questioned me, and I'd forgotten where the line of inquiry inevitably led.

Patrice's playful insistence that I had sex with the unnamed masters left me puzzled. "Come now, not once?"

I assured, "No, never."

She was in good-natured doubt, grinning, asking like we were best friends, "Have you ever?"

I thought it made me look unsophisticated to be twenty-three and inexperienced. Virginity was a hindrance to my image I wouldn't admit. I was coy, "Of course, there were others."

Patrice leaned forward smiling. "Who?"

"An occasional friend of the master."

It was all clear to her now. "You had sex with the masters' *friends*. Ahhh ..." Then without warning, "Were you forced?"

"*No.*" But I was once more utterly mystified why the issue of sex kept coming up, and now it was veering into rape. Blessed hell, no one had any respect for masters of craft. Not that I had said what any of them held a mastery of, but wow, adults were really obsessed with who was going to bed with whom, and they'd just frankly ask you who you'd slept with. Amazing, if not a little disconcerting.

It was 1985 and what young teenagers knew about sex was limited to what you or your friends could either gather or glimpse when you were strictly not meant to. I had been the first in my class to know much of anything. I had learned about this, too, from a book. I had found it on the shelves of the public library, right next to Emily Brontë, but unmarked by the library's filing system, and I knew by the end of the first page it didn't belong. The back cover still had the sticker price which revealed it had come from Nashville's Biggest Adult Bookstore. I had no idea adults had their very own exclusive book store, but fanning through the pages, I could see why. Slipping it under my sweater, I had secreted it home, and then read it from start to finish in a night.

The next day at school, I was eager to share my newfound wisdom. My description of the acts described in the book attracted a growing group of spellbound girls. Circled around the largest library table, I explained the whole carnal thing and concluded by telling them, "At the end, something comes out of the man called come. But it's spelled C - U - M. Cum. It's white."

Never before had I held so many people's undivided and absolutely rapt attention.

But then one girl decided this cum nonsense was just one inexplicable thing too many and declared, "Nuh-uh, that doesn't happen," and then everyone else concurred. With steadfast conviction, they all sat back and denied it was possible, thinking this was either a terrible misunderstanding on my part, or I was just making it up.

But I hadn't even told them what was particularly astonishing, so to give myself credibility, because I had read this in a book and, therefore, knew it to be true, I told them, "The woman mostly swallows it."

Now everyone was revolted. Over the sound of a dozen girls groaning in disgust, my biggest critic asked me, "Why are you telling us this?"

"Because we all need to know it. I mean really, this is going to be expected of us in a few years." Finally, I imparted, "It happens a lot at funerals." That is what the book said, that women got "very horny" at death and every man knew it. The men in the book crossed the country attending funerals and consoling young widows.

And that was pretty much the extent of my knowledge in Dallas.

I wasn't fully comfortable admitting I had gotten up to any of the antics mentioned in the book, so every time Patrice brought up sex, I'd roll, tighten, or contort my lips against the thought of what I'd read. It wasn't a subject Patrice could get very far with.

She switched topics, asking outright, "Do you believe you were the victim of white slavery?"

"Slavery?" It was the first time I had heard the term applied to me.

Patrice explained how it could look as such, "You've described being used as a companion to men you only knew as master. Though you've traveled throughout the world, you can't say where exactly because your activities were too closely restricted. You were essentially confined to the house. Do you not think this was a form of slavery?"

"I don't know," but I wanted to fix it. In every interview, be it with law enforcement or here with Patrice, I had meant it to appear I was lying when I said I didn't know the names or locations of the people I stayed with. I had made all the appropriate expressions: I'd broken eye contact and looked off to the side, then had lowered my voice to become uncomfortably reticent and curt with answers. I'd thought I'd played it brilliantly obvious. But Patrice was telling me it was the opinion of investigators that I had been used as a slave.

I understood my mistake.

I'd been actively experimenting with deception for several years. One of the things I seemed to intuitively know was to allow people to convince themselves. Hold back and they would fill in what most appealed to them. I rarely explained myself or made excuses because the best excuse was the one the accuser made for themselves. Let them explain. And I knew better than to try to sway their opinion. Such actions caused friction and you didn't want to slow anyone down when they were headlong committed to persuading themselves.

It was a strategy that had served me very well. And it hadn't exactly failed me in Dallas; it had just taken me in an unexpected direction.

Patrice asked, "Do you believe you were a slave?"

I'm quoted in the newspaper as saying, "I'm not going to say positively yes, or no."

"So it's possible?"

"Anything is possible." It just wasn't agreeable.

~~~~~~

It was December and Patrice's article ran in the Sunday edition of the *Austin American Statesman*. The title was: "Shrouded past of 'countess' leads to lost existence in Collin County." It told the story as so many agencies had heard it but was punctuated with quotes from Rick, Mike, and a US spokesman for Interpol.

A common view repeated throughout the article was spoken by Rick: "I've really had mixed emotions about it. There are some times when you stop and think about the story and it's completely outlandish. And there are other times when you listen to this girl talk and you watch her mannerisms and it's very believable."

The article was impartial to my tale, giving the facts and then reminding the reader a state psychiatric hospital had found me sane. It described me as polished and articulate though not particularly forthcoming when pressed for details. It highlighted investigators' attempts to trip me up, yet I continued to repeat my story again and again without flaw. Patrice either didn't know, or kindly omitted, I had given my real name while being screamed awake in the mental ward. And the article concluded with the general opinion given by Mike: "I want to believe her and I want to help her. But I don't believe the entire story. I think there's more to the story than we know about."

It was left up to the reader to decide if the story I told was true, or alternatively, that I might be "a deeply disturbed, very capable liar." What it did not leave open to debate was that I had been "a slave to wealthy masters throughout the world."

I read it once and couldn't bear to see it again. I didn't want to be a slave, and I still hadn't figured out it was a sex slave, which would have disturbed me considerably more. Patrice had been incredibly kind and more than fair, but to ensure no one saw it, especially Sergiu and Daniel, the article had to be buried in the trash.

FLIRTING WITH VIOLENCE

I'd never had a boyfriend, and I'd never been kissed. I'd done quite a bit of flirting before leaving Tennessee, and I knew how to subtly tease older men into a fever, but I had no one to retreat behind in Dallas, and I didn't dare play that trick alone. And as far as I could see, there wasn't anyone to play it on.

Sergiu was more than twice my real age but he didn't have the lascivious eyes I was familiar with. He didn't look like the men in Tennessee, the ones who showed such palpable interest that I just had to lure them back to my father. My father was a WWII Marine veteran that no one dared cross, but he would still say to my mother, "I'm going to spend my last days beating them off her with a stick." And it was all kinds of funny because I knew I was safe.

I wasn't about to rile anyone up in Dallas without protection. Save for the ten-minute charge in the Corvette, I was in all ways modest and reserved.

And Sergiu was a friend.

I viewed him with an astounding level of ignorance, not at all recognizing that what we were doing was considered dating, or that having been out with him so many times implied a certain interest, which I didn't have.

At first I thought I was a burden that Daniel had dumped on him to clear the way to Tricia, and after a while, I assumed Sergiu had simply grown fond of me. By the end of January, I also knew he loved sharing meals with me.

He said, "You like my private dinner theater. You sit and show starts."

This was true. I had a young mastery of the evening meal, and to ensure I remained Sergiu's favorite guest, I performed. I knew how to make charming conversation about the news, wildlife, outer space, and a thousand other eclectic topics I had collected from books. My family's dinners had always been an open exchange of ideas and recently acquired information, and as a family, we had known each other forever, so tedious background inquiries were never part of the discussion.

With the same familiarity, I conversed with Sergiu, wholly avoiding the mundane details of personal histories. The general topics allowed both of us to keep any questions from falling on our past. I knew absolutely nothing of Sergiu's life before Dallas, and he knew nothing of mine. We neither asked nor revealed.

Tonight we were talking about the infamous 1976 Société Générale bank heist in France. A gang of militants, con artists, and assassins had tunneled through the sewers into the vault. Over the long Bastille holiday, they'd had a bit of a party clearing out the jewels, gold bullion, and cash in the safety deposit boxes.

"Albert Spaggiari," Sergiu dipped his head in respect to the man who had devised the plan. We laughed over his escape from court. "Spaggiari say, 'Judge look at this,' and then," Sergiu held his hands together to imitate a dive, "right out the window."

"Three stories," I confirmed.

"No hurt."

"He knew how to fall. He used to sky dive."

"Ah?" Sergiu hadn't known that, but he knew something better. "They say the man waiting with motorbike was French minister."

"Really? Oh, that's funny."

"Spaggiari live free all his life in Argentina. He have very good girlfriend. She no talk."

We both agreed that the break-in had been brilliant, but I particularly respected what the thieves had written on the vault's wall. I quoted it to Sergiu, "Without weapons, nor hatred, nor violence."

Sergiu waved it away. Their passive creed was inconsequential to him. He was more impressed with the haul. "Maybe thirty million," the balance of his hands tipped low. "Or maybe hundred million," the scales weighed high. "Me? I be happy with either."

~~~~~~

It had been a typical and lively exchange, but once the meal was over, so was the show. The table was the stage and I was an actor at a dinner theater, totally on script while food was present, engaging and attentive, enthralled by every subject, but once the stage was left behind, I was off, gone behind the curtain, too coldly removed for Sergiu to enjoy.

Back in the latest Audi, Sergiu considered my aloof disposition and said, "You no make this," and dropped his hand over his face to leave only the faint smile and coma eyes he mocked as my expression. "Tonight, I keep you happy."

He had moved out of the shabby apartment to a townhouse with a garage. "But you no tell Tricia. She think I live with Daniel and Eugene. Yes?"

"Yes, of course." I moved through the rooms barely breathing. It smelled new and synthetic. The furniture was still black leather but bigger, and the tables were black enamel trimmed in metallic gold. Gaudy gold mirrors and framed oil paintings were nearly everywhere. Then, things turned beige. The windows and sliding patio door were covered in vertical blinds, and new Berber carpet abutted taupe painted walls. The neutral tones managed to make the furnishings just that little extra bit vulgar so the whole place felt harsh and jarring.

The bottle of champagne Sergiu was taking from the refrigerator took an already uncomfortable scene and ran it straight for the cliffs. I didn't realize I was backing toward the door until Sergiu asked, "Where you going?"

Afraid I might reveal myself as unsophisticated, because I was certain no worldly woman would be alarmed by anything that was occurring, I smiled away any thought of retreat and took a seat in the corner of the couch.

When Sergiu gave me a bubbling champagne glass, I put it on the coffee table and he handed it back. I held it explaining, "I've never cared for it."

"I bring this for you, from New York."

"Oh." I tipped the glass to my lips but consumed nothing, then said, "Thank you," and held it like a prop.

Sergiu laughed. He asked suspiciously, "You drink?"

"Yes," I was smiling assurance.

He didn't believe me, sat down flush next to me so that the smell of leather and patchouli, the distinct heavy scent of Givenchy, was wrapping around me. He pressed, "Show me you drink."

I pushed back into the arm of the couch and he followed. I warned, "Sergiu ..."

And he said, "My name no Sergiu."

Really? How very interesting. I forgot to finish my appeal for restraint.

"Ah," he chuckled, "now you give me eyes."

I was smirking, expectantly waiting to hear the rest, but he wasn't moving or speaking, just grinning and waiting like me until I was finally forced to ask, "Then how did you get the name, the identity, all the paperwork and passport?"

My question surprised him. He was expecting to hear me ask for his real name. He appeared slightly hurt and disconcerted, saying, "Is name of Romanian."

"Yes, I know. You have travel documents. How did you get the name?" The question of how to acquire genuine, federally recognized identity completely possessed me, and whatever-his-name could see it.

With a little bit of concern, he sat back to call me, "Demonia."

"Yes, yes," I was getting vexed and brushed it aside with hurried aggravation. "Madonna, demonia, my mamma mia, you're Italian. How did you get Romanian documents?" Then seeing I was causing offense, I tried to undo it by sipping at the champagne.

He gave a little, "I work in Romania. I drive from Italia for my family."

I was smiling encouragement, taking another small swallow.

"I know a man. He no so good."

I turned my head for explanation and took another sip.

"No so good here," he touched his heart.

I frowned, "A bad person? Criminal?"

"Bad here," again the heart.

"Sick?"

"Yes. He no so good. He no stay long. We agree. I take his name."

"Did he die?"

"Ah," he rolled it around not willing to confirm it.

I took another drink. "There'd be a body. A death certificate. A grave …"

"Ah," turning his head, "maybe no."

No book had ever captivated or intrigued me like this. I was completely enthralled, trying to put it together, absently raising the glass to my mouth and then scowling with disgust to taste the Chardonnay grape, but never mind that, I wanted to know, "Did you just go get a driver's license in his name? Or communist papers? Did they not have a picture on file?"

He wasn't answering, so I tried the drink trick again. He rolled his eyes, shook his head, said, "Stop," and nearly laughed. "You no like," he took the glass from my hand and put it back on the table. "I have his work book," he opened his hands like the pages were large.

"Picture," he licked the imaginary image like a stamp and slapped it into one hand. "Same with military book."

"And then?"

He was pressing me into the arm of the couch again, but I was spellbound and hardly noticed until he put his hand on the back of my neck, preventing me from withdrawing further. He brushed his lips over mine, testing my resistance, but I was waiting to hear how it was done, so let him force a kiss on me to hear him say, "I go home," then blocked his hand from my breast while he continued, "I say to asylum camp, 'I am Român. My name is Sergiu.'" I was ducking to the side when he said, "I speak romaneste. Is no problem."

It sounded sublimely simple, making me think I had really messed things up in my attempt to get new identification. And it was too late for me now; the sheriff's department, the FBI, DEA, and Interpol all had my fingerprints. I was tearing everything apart in my head, trying to figure out if there was a way I could fix it, or a way to backtrack and attach it, wondering who in the world would do a similar thing for me, thinking hard when the imposter pressing down on me said, "You no ask why."

It occurred to me I hadn't. I turned my face back to him with interest.

"But you no ask. Why you no ask?"

"I'm asking now. Tell me why." He got his arm behind my back and worked to shift me down while I pushed against his chest, smirking, shaking my head to deny him, yet still wanting an answer. "Tell me."

He began whispering a story in my ear that convinced me I should never have turned my face back, and if I hoped to reach sixteen, I'd better extricate myself and forget. I started saying, "Okay, that's enough," to both the tale and his advancements. Both continued. "No, no, no," I was trying to keep it light and frivolous, "That's more than I require." But there was more. "Okay, really, time for this to end." Except it didn't.

"I want to hear you say my name."

"Sure," I was pushing myself to the side, reaching for the coffee table, leaning for the floor. "Tell me what it is."

Something about the way I said it didn't settle right with him. He yanked me back, shaking his head, annoyed, on the cusp of becoming angry. His expression was irritated but his voice was formal, "What is your name?"

It sounded like it came out of an English phrase book. I thought he wanted me to reword my question, so I spoke with indulgence, "Fine. What is your name?"

"No. What is your name?"

I nearly repeated it again with sincerity before realizing he was asking me. I reached for the top of the couch, trying to pull myself up, laughing it away. "You know my name."

"No," and he slammed me back into the cushions. "I think about this. You no care my name. You only want to know how I get name Sergiu. You want new name with passport. You tell me," his hand was tightening around my neck, "what is your name?"

This was not expected. I stopped moving, returned my face to dead calm with coma eyes, except this time there was no hint of a

108

smile. I looked down over my body under his with contempt and asked, "Would you like to get off me now?"

The confrontation took a moment but he finally looked away, removed his hand from my throat, started to shift, and I shifted as well. Then he was enraged again and it all went back to the way it was and he was demanding, "What is your name?"

"Jesus," I said, and got choked for the sacrilege. "Not my name," I explained, "God," and got choked again. "Seriously now, dammit, stop." *Christ*.

"What is your name?"

"You know my name."

"What is your name?"

"Constance. You know that."

"I tell you my name. My name is …"

"*No!* No, no, no," I did not want to hear. I was trying to pry his hand off my throat saying, "If this is going to escalate into a tit for tat, you should know I have nothing to offer, so this needs to stop before it starts." I thought the scene was turning around when he released my neck, but he was only wrestling one of my arms behind my back to be trapped by our combined weight and the back of the couch, the other he held over my head while I insisted, "My name is Constance."

He was pulling to get the length of my skirt up, saying, "My name is Marco." And then getting his hand beneath the material to cup between my legs, "What is your name?"

~~~~~

I tried angry demands for him to stop followed by cold emotionless calls for him to recognize what he was doing, and then, finally, I resorted to begging, but nothing I said stopped it from happening, and through it all, he continued to ask, "What is your name?" But I knew the truth wouldn't have made any difference either.

At a certain point, I realized the goal had changed, and now the objective was to just get through it with as much dignity as I could preserve. It became a matter of endurance.

When it was finally over and I was pulling myself back together, he looked down at his hand and wanted to know, "You menstruate?"

As if I wasn't embarrassed enough, he wanted to talk about my cycle. I kept shifting my clothes around and was about to walk off when he pulled me into his lap to put his hand under my skirt again, between my legs, rummaging around to confirm the blood was mine. He asked a second time, "You menstruate?"

I was struggling to get up, fighting to get his hands off me, but he held me in his lap and asked again.

I admitted, "No."

"You virgin?"

"Not after that."

My back was against his chest and I felt him take it like a punch, a great winding that left his lungs empty and made him gasp. Then he was kind, trying to hug me, console me, whispering something that sounded like regret, and I was freaking out, twisting and recoiling for the floor, preferring the violence to whatever this was, strangling a sound close to a scream, just wanting to get away.

On the floor now, I was kneeling with his hand too tight on my shoulder, hurting me so I wouldn't go any further, but his words were pleading; and I didn't want to move, didn't want to see or have it confirmed that he might be crying.

I said, "Okay, everybody calm down. We're all adults," and then laughed at my joke. "This is a simple matter. Just go get me a washcloth. A wet towel. Whatever. Bring me something from the bathroom."

And as soon as he was in the hall, I was at the door, and when the water started to run, I was slipping quietly out to open the garage.

The door to the Audi slammed too loud in the small space and the smell of Givenchy was overpowering to the point of disturbing. I fought a moment of panic not to get back out and slam the car door a second time. But getting caught again, embraced again, that would be so much worse. I turned the keyless ignition, and the engine was louder still, unnerving me further. Then reverse was a grinding nightmare and the tires squealed when the gas and clutch didn't match going into first, but I was in the street, finding second, then third, speeding off down the road to reach a hundred, finally able to relax, even smile again, thinking this stolen car was pretty damn thrilling, and also damn pretty. It was nearly a shame I was going to have to destroy it.

A Little Aside

Until we conclude with Dallas, my every excuse is going to be a singular: Fifteen.

I was fifteen and had no freaking idea what was going on. I was fifteen and had not yet developed a clear sense of myself or others or what was permissible, and even when I knew something wasn't acceptable, I had no idea how to assert my authority because I was fifteen.

As we continue from this point, you might find yourself clamping your hands to your head and exclaiming, *"What the fuck? Why did you think that was an appropriate reaction?"*

And my answer will be, "Fifteen."

You will be expecting some justification for my perceived indifference, perhaps asking, "Why the hell didn't you go to the police?"

But my answer will still be, "Fifteen."

We should come to the understanding now that things will move along at a better pace if you just accept my answer is always going to be "Fifteen," and then I won't have to stop and explain that my every ridiculous action was because I was an inexperienced fifteen-year-old sociopath who had never had any depth of emotion.

You might insist I explain, "But why would you ever allow him back in your presence again?"

But it's still going to be, "Fifteen."

"You kept speaking to him. What the hell was with that?"

"Fifteen."

"Why did you not call out for help?"

"Fifteen."

"And why? Why after all *that* did you then decide to threaten him?"

"Fifteen."

"Were you fucking crazy?"

"A little, but I was also fifteen."

Destroy Them All

There's a trick to utterly destroying a car without hurting yourself. I discovered it by accident trying to smash the Audi's headlights into the corner of a brick grocery store. You can rather easily tear away all the mirrors and bumpers and doors, and really just about everything that makes a car attractive, by hooking them on the corner of a sturdy building and then staying on the gas until you rip it screeching off. And those big metal dumpsters are pretty hilarious, too. Donut into those a few times and you can do amazing things to the fenders. Vacillating between the two procedures will quickly turn a top dollar car into such a ravaged and shapeless heap of indistinguishable parts that even the most seasoned insurance adjuster will flinch to see it.

The only thing I couldn't figure out was how to completely tear off the hood, but as it was, I figured my work stood for itself. Before the remaining dented fenders prevented the tires from spinning, I limped it three houses down from Tricia's, wiped it of fingerprints, and left it on the street for Sergiu to find.

I spent the next day hiding in the library, and by the time Rick picked me up for dinner, the Audi was gone.

There had been an interesting new development in my case that Rick wanted to discuss. He had been investigating ways to obtain a green card for me so I could work, but first I would need a residence visa. As it stood, I was not legally allowed to remain in the United

States but Immigration didn't know where to deport me either. Lest they be forced to take me into custody, the INS agents advised Rick not to stir anything up.

But that was hardly a satisfactory solution to Rick, and as he alone had been left to resolve it, he went instead to the ACLU. The biggest problem was I could not give a date or location of birth, so I would never be able to produce a birth certificate. The only way the lawyers could foresee someone in my position legally working or living in the United States was for Congress to declare me a resident. The situation was so unique, the ACLU agreed to represent me. When the lower house next convened, the lawyers hoped a vote would decide my legal status. The move would set a precedent.

I kept a straight and serious face but I wanted to laugh. Sergiu's ruse had nothing on mine.

"Only one small problem though," Rick looked a little disturbed. "Your age is making it difficult. The ACLU said it would go more smoothly if you entered the country as a minor. I think you can pass for eighteen. Do you think that would be okay?"

Now I did laugh, but Rick couldn't guess why. I said, "I have no issue with it."

And though he was the one to suggest it, he didn't appear entirely comfortable with the decision. He looked around the restaurant like someone could be watching and confessed, "With you now eighteen, this dinner might be a little inappropriate."

~~~~~

Sergiu was angry with himself for being asleep when Rick dropped me off. He'd had a busy day dealing with the mess I'd made of the Audi, and he'd meant to learn who this detective was that Tricia had mentioned.

He knew the name was Rick, but Tricia couldn't remember if Rick was with the police or the sheriff's department, much less what division he represented, and his last name had slipped her mind right after she'd heard it.

I'd noticed an expensive red BMW was parked around the corner and knew either Daniel was spending the night or Sergiu was waiting.

I was hoping it was Sergiu because I had an evil grin just for him.

He was laid back across the center of my bed, unaware until I dropped my head next to his and whispered, "Were your friends in New York terribly mad?"

It was stupid. I saw that immediately.

I didn't have time to retreat before he had a hand full of my hair and had wound it in his fist. "Who is Rick?" He was rising up, pulling me from the opposite edge with him.

I didn't want a scene that was going to draw in Tricia, but the pain gripping my hair and the discomfort of being twisted across the bed made me angry. I was growling low, "Let go. I mean it, let me go."

He'd pulled himself to sit upright and had dragged me down beside him. I knew the back of his hand was turning bloody because my nails were in his flesh, but he didn't react. He just took it and said, "You no hurt me," then tightened his grip until I was wincing, "Okay, okay," and stopped.

"Who is Rick?"

"No."

"Who is Rick?" He wrenched at the coil he'd made of my hair until I put my nails back into his hand and went for his face with my other. He knocked the attack aside and pinned my wrist to the bed, asking, "Rick?"

He dealt with the blood I was clawing from his hand by tearing at my scalp until I conceded again, "Okay, okay, I've stopped."

"Who is Rick?"

"No."

He gave a disappointed shake of his head and then started pulling harder at my hair, waiting for me to gasp so he could ask again, "Rick?"

Before he made me scream, I gave in, admitting, "A detective. Stop, he's a detective."

"With the police?"

"Yes."

"What is his name?"

"Rick."

"What is his name?"

A vicious tug convinced me to lie further, "I don't know his last name."

"What is his name?"

"I don't know."

"Name?"

"I swear, I don't know. I can't even remember yours."

"What is your name?"

I looked at him worried, afraid of where this was going.

"You make much trouble for me. You tell me, what is your name?"

"It's Constance. You know that."

But he shook his head, unconvinced, and twisted his fist again.

Trying to pry his hand lose, I was pleading with sounds of pain until he relented enough for me to speak again. "You can rip my damn hair out, it's still going to be Constance."

"You tell Rick about me?"

"No."

"Why you with Rick?"

"He's trying to get me a green card."

"How?"

Of all the things, I did not want to say how that was meant to happen. I was trying to think of an answer, but in the quiet pause, I was fairly certain he had wrenched my hair until my scalp was bleeding. I blurted out, "Congress is going to vote on it."

"*What?*"

That sounded so absurd, I couldn't say it twice. I said instead, "You have to let go." The back of my head felt hot and damp, and whether it was from the sweat of his hand or my blood, I couldn't tell, but he felt it too and changed his pressure to my wrist. I started turning with the stress, rambling, "Okay, stop, the ACLU, it's complicated, ow, Jesus, no sorry, oh God, ow, I didn't mean that, wait, it's paperwork. I swear, it's just a great deal of paperwork."

"You no so good with truth," he seemed saddened by it. "Now you tell me, what is your name?"

He was tossing aside the long fabric of my skirt, reaching between my legs again, and I was begging, "Oh please don't," regretting the hilarious question about his friends in New York, but already certain they'd never see that expensive red BMW either.

$$\sim\sim\sim\sim\sim$$

And so it went. Once a week Sergiu would come for dinner, and when Tricia went to bed with Daniel, Sergiu would back step me into my room where failed coercion would lead to force. And then, when he fell asleep, I'd take his car and rip it apart on the corner of a building.

He was angry. His friends in New York were angrier. I was costing them all a lot of money.

I told him, "Then stop. Stop pinning me to the bed, and you'll stop losing your cars."

Three totaled luxury cars in, and he arrived to overpower me in an old Ford Pinto. I laughed at the attempt. Taking his set of keys, I drove the Pinto to his house and reversed a Jaguar out of the garage. While I was out, I had a spare key made to his townhouse then, missing one door and dragging the other, the body shredded down to dangling electronics, I forced the Jaguar back into the garage and parked the undamaged Pinto in front of Tricia's house.

I was laughing to myself as I went to sleep on the couch. Imagining his smug victory when he saw the Pinto undamaged was amusing, but funnier still was what waited for him at home.

He was gone when I left for the library and I knew I wouldn't see him for several days. He had plans to drive that night with Eugene, Daniel, and half a dozen new Eastern Bloc recruits to New York with a small fleet of cars, so when Rick called telling me there was something new we should discuss, I was unconcerned Sergiu would learn I had gone to dinner with him again.

My concern was with Rick. I had heard it in his voice on the phone, a tone that was on the stiff side of professional, and then when he arrived, he was tense. At the restaurant, he kept his distance.

Something had gone wrong, and I was at my most appealing to smooth it over. But I couldn't keep the conversation frivolously pleasant all evening. The dinner plates were cleared and we were drinking wine when he told me my file had been sent back to Interpol. He'd been requested to do it when I abruptly changed from twenty-three to eighteen. As a matter of routine, the organization searched three years to either side of a person's listed age, but now there was a five-year difference, they wanted to look again. And so did the FBI. And the same three-year allowance had been followed with the missing persons search through America's fifty states.

Starting to feel sick with dread, I was waiting to hear Rick say I resembled a runaway from Tennessee. My nerves were about to shriek when it occurred to me that if the detective suspected such a thing, he would never have allowed me a drink. But it was still out there, a pending disaster that could drop any day on his desk.

I wanted to ask, but didn't dare, yet I had to know. I went at it sideways, "Running my details again in the United States will make no difference, but I will be interested to know what Interpol discovers."

"We both know you're not eighteen. Interpol won't find anything, and I'm not searching missing persons in the US again."

I nodded agreement, saying, "Of course," rejoicing, thanking the fates that kept letting me slip through.

He started to summarize, "So, the ACLU has your file, and Interpol and the FBI are examining it again."

"This is all quite excellent," I was smiling gratitude, still trying to break through the business mood.

But his manner remained the same. He said, "I received a call from Ron Howard."

I waited to hear who he was.

"He's a well-known film director. He wants to make a movie about your life."

It was the sort of thing that should have made me laugh, but it didn't. Dinner theater with its pleasing dialogue came to an abrupt end. The curtain was down. The show over. Every light in the house extinguished.

I wanted to smile and be obliging, but I felt like the movie was going to be expected of me, and I instantly detested it. My single goal was to possess the lovely title of countess and valid identification.

That Congress was going to vote to give it to me was delightfully funny, but something about a movie seemed crude, and more than anything, I did not want to be turned into a spectacle.

I wouldn't say yes or no or anything to Rick about Ron Howard. I wanted no part of it, but I also didn't want to openly refuse something Rick brought to me, especially when I thought he was in favor of it, so I just nodded that I had heard, then stared at him blankly when he pressed for a response.

"Should I tell him you're interested?"

Silence.

"You understand what this means?"

I could hear a waitress scooping ice into a glass.

"They will probably offer you a lot of money."

And more distant, pots were clanging in the kitchen.

"They could make you famous."

I looked to see what the table next to us was doing.

For the first time in the evening, Rick laughed and relaxed. He had dealt with me long enough to recognize my vacuous expression and steadfast silence was a passive refusal to cooperate, and this time he was happy to receive it.

Early on he had come to feel responsible for me. He had acquired my file while I was still under observation at the first psychiatric hospital, and he had driven me out to the Falls when I was committed. He had an assumption about the scar on my wrist and the meaning of the word master, and he did not want my past used for entertainment.

Our reasons to be against it arrived at the same position from different paths, but they were both driven by a strong sense of decorum.

He said, "I'll take care of it," and I turned the lights back on.

~~~~~~

I was probably only asleep for thirty minutes when I woke up with the realization that someone was sitting beside me on the bed. I could smell him. For explanation, I asked, "Sergiu?"

"You no say my name. Why? You know my name, but you no say Marco. You say Sergiu."

"I thought you were going to New York."

"Something happen with Jaguar. Maybe you know. It has no doors."

I quietly laughed at the way he mentioned it.

"I have new car. I go soon. But first I tell you: You see Rick again, I kill him."

I sat up and warned, "You will get the electric chair."

"The *what*?"

"Texas will execute you."

"No."

"Yes. He's a cop. You will get the death penalty."

"No," he shook his head in the dark, condescension chuckling in his throat as though I were the clueless one. "Five years, ten most," he tossed it away as trivial.

"When you get to New York, ask your friends to tell you what happens to cop killers in the United States. Even better, you ask them about the death penalty in Texas. And then, when you come back, you tell me what you think."

He stood and remained motionless for several moments while I listened to his aggravated breath. Huffing out frustration, he turned and leaned down as though he were going to kiss me goodbye but stopped when I recoiled. He left, saying flatly, "You see him again, I kill him."

UNWANTED ATTENTION

Days later, with Sergiu still in New York, I went to his townhouse and used the spare key I had made.

I searched through the cabinets and drawers, pushing aside the collection of filed down car keys, but slipping into my purse a receipt to a Dallas parking garage, his phone bill, and some New York addresses scribbled on ripped out phonebook pages. There was no clear plan in my mind on what I intended. I went looking to see what there was, and I took what I did because I thought it could be useful.

When I returned home, Tricia was eager to see me. "I just spoke with two of Ron Howard's assistants. They want to make a movie about you!"

I could not imagine how they had found her, but she wasn't delivering any more of that news to me. I retreated into my head to board up the house and tack on a vacant sign.

She caught me fleeing out the back. "If you can give them enough material, they want to film a three-part television drama."

I hadn't expected it to get worse. I knew Tricia was still talking but I was gone, remembering every midweek made-for-television movie that had ever chased me from the living room into a book. They were all so earnest, and depressing, and something worse that I couldn't quite place except they induced pity, like the doctor clucking over my wrist, and I truly could not bear the thought of it.

My con was already going horribly wrong. I was going to be better known as a slave than a countess. What was worse, everyone who knew anything about my story treated me with sad sympathy. It mattered not the least that I was practically always smiling. And it was sincere; I was happy as long as Sergiu wasn't holding me down. But no one knew about that, so the somber, delicate manner people assumed with me was disconcerting, and I imagined after a three-part miniseries, strangers would clutch my hand and weep.

The best way to deal with it was to ignore it. It would stop.

But Ron Howard's assistants kept calling, and Tricia entered negotiations with them on my behalf. As soon as I was told, "You'll spend at least two weeks, possibly even two months, with a writer going over the details of your life," I started sabotaging the assistants' attempts. The phone kept mysteriously being unplugged, the wires frayed, the cord lost.

When they managed to get through, I'd back away from the phone like three of Sergiu's brothers had just called for a date.

I had spent maybe three hours with Patrice from the *Austin American Statesman* and within thirty minutes, I felt more thoroughly interrogated than I had in all the FBI, DEA, sheriff, and psychological interviews combined. My story was abstract, amounting to little more than great colorful swipes of a brush on a black canvas. I could smile, act coy, or look away when Patrice broached an unknown or uncomfortable topic, but she hadn't paid for it. Ron Howard was planning to pay, and I didn't imagine my stubborn silence over the details would be accepted.

And for all the trouble, the price was far from compelling. His company was offering fifteen thousand dollars for the rights to film, stage, books, songs, all print, including newspapers and magazines, quotes and interviews, then, in case they missed something, any and all media for the duration of my life, past and bloody future.

Tricia thought it was great, telling me, "You can buy a brand new Pontiac Fiero."

I nearly choked. "If I'm going to get raped like that, I at least expect a Porsche."

I offended myself with the joke, but Tricia had little idea of what was happening with Sergiu. I pleaded in hushed tones, afraid to make a scene, and then silently endured it. Tricia had heard it only once, lingering outside my room, hearing me repeat no, and please no. She had mimicked me the next day over morning coffee, saying, "No, Sergiu, stop. Please, Sergiu, don't." It seemed grievously cruel. I couldn't breathe for fending off the numerous ways the mockery stabbed me in the chest, but her focus was in the newspaper and she shook her head with amused acceptance, saying, "I went to bed when I heard you laugh."

She thought my no was a fetish yes.

And I knew exactly what had been so funny. Wrist shackled to the frame of the bed, I had been taking a mental inventory of my bedside drawer with its scattering of hairpins, safety pens, and paperclips. I'd known since I was twelve how pick handcuffs, so I'd found genuine humor in Sergiu's assertion, "You no take my car tonight."

COSTLY MISTAKE

Sergiu was accustomed to saying, "Come, we go to dinner," and having me obediently comply, but I hadn't done that since tearing apart the first Audi. He'd say, "Come," and I'd shake my head and put it back in a book. I could say no to dinner out, but I didn't think I had the right to tell him he couldn't be in the house. It wasn't my house, and Daniel was paying the bills.

They'd still take over the kitchen, and he'd call for me to join them, shouting cheerfully into the living room, "Constanzia, come, I show you little fish," as though he were still the same mirthful guest, utterly safe, holding no ill intent toward me whatsoever.

When I didn't respond, he came to wrap his hand around the back of my neck and whisper, "I no touch you. Everything is good. You come." And I believed him. We all had a marvelous evening, but after it was over, he didn't keep his word, so I had to rip the doors off another Jaguar.

The next time he was driving a Porsche, so he kept his distance. But the following week, he brought the Pinto again, and when I got to his townhouse, there was nothing in his garage. I was tired and the Ford hardly seemed worth the effort. I'd also been warned that Pinto's were prone to explode, so I left it in a ditch.

Then, there was the mystery car.

Sergiu came to plead with me on the couch, cajoling, "I be good with you. I leave after dinner," hand over heart. "You be my dinner theater and I no touch." But I'd heard it before and was shaking my head. He continued, "You come and start show, I bring you something from New York. Yes?"

The last time he'd brought a Bvlgari watch but I'd refused to take it. It was ugly, and I wasn't fond of keeping up with the time. But I was curious what he'd bring next, so I asked, "After dinner, you promise to leave?"

He cut his hand through the air to underscore it, "I no touch you."

But he did. And outside was the Pinto again. And his garage was empty.

But he was going to New York, so there was a car somewhere.

I knew he was violent, but I wasn't afraid of him. I was resentful. I felt put-upon. And after so many assurances, I was in a crazy state of rage. I was looking around his townhouse thinking there were many things I could destroy, but it was all so trivial. None of it had the scope or complexity of demolishing a car that was expected in New York.

I went out to search the few vehicles parked on the street, but all their doors were locked. The doors on Sergiu's cars were never locked. They opened without resistance and the ignition turned either without a key or with any key.

In a moment of insight, it occurred to me where the car was, but I couldn't remember the address. I searched the drawer under his phone for another monthly receipt to the parking garage and then took the collection of filed down car keys.

The multilevel car park was in a business district. It was nearly 3:00 a.m. and the place was dimly lit but empty. It took me an hour to find the car whose doors weren't locked. It was under a fitted tarp that was tied to the front and rear bumper. It wasn't coming off easily, so I only worked on one side. At first glance, I thought it was a mint condition '68 Mustang, but once I got the tarp half removed, I changed my mind and considered it might be a new design for the Mazda RX7. It was neither and I didn't recognize the winged emblem on the hood.

Sitting in it, I was certain it was expensive though. The ignition switch was in the dash but none of the keys from Sergiu's drawer would start the engine. The keys would turn from vertical to horizontal, but then nothing happened. It gave me a terrible feeling. I covered my mouth and sheepishly whispered, "Oh sorry," to whoever the owner was. Tying the tarp back around the bumpers, I spent another hour looking for a car with unlocked doors. There were two. Neither worth the trouble of taking to New York and their ignitions didn't turn.

I went back to the mystery car. Sitting in the driver's seat the first time, I had thought it was me that smelled like Sergiu. I couldn't seem to scrub the scent out of my skin. Everything smelled like Givenchy. It was in my room, in my clean sheets, and my pillow kept returning it to my hair. I'd turn a corner in the house and it was on the wall, on the couch, in my books. I couldn't imagine what had ever been appealing about the scent. It was aggressive and heavy and suffocating. And it was in the mystery car. The scent was cold, not like what was rising from my skin. It smelled different. I put my face into the driver's seat to confirm it.

It made me want to return the violence.

I used the filed down keys again, trying to turn the ignition, but it wouldn't come to life. There had to be a trick, and I was searching for it. I didn't think I'd find it in the glove box, but I discovered a photocopy of an ad with the car's emblem. It was an Aston Martin. It meant little to me except now it had a name. I fanned through the maps, an oil change book, and several restaurant menus, but there was no registration or insurance to tell me the age or model of the car.

I passed my attention briefly over the dash and then down the steering column. I had seen countless actors reach under the driver's dash to hotwire a car and hoped to find two obviously exposed wires, but instead of wires, I knocked loose a small black box with a button.

It absolutely terrified me.

I knew I'd have to push it, but I didn't want to. I hated being startled. I was hard to scare but easy to startle, and I was afraid the button was going to set off alarms.

The first noise surprised me into releasing the button and dropping the box, but it was an overreaction. The engine turned on the second attempt.

I had thought destroying the Jaguar in Sergiu's garage had been the most sneaky, thrilling thing ever, but the Aston Martin hidden in the parking garage beat everything else. Sergiu was going to flip. I was laughing imaging his face when he started peeling back the tarp. He'd know instantly I had done it. He'd see the black paint on

131

the central column between the second and third level and he'd know I had driven it up and down the ramp, running the sides into the concrete. He'd see the glass shattered on the ground where it was parked and know I had run it repeatedly into the wall, forward and reverse, headlights and brake lights, and when I was done, I'd kicked the muffler under the chassis. It wasn't the most devastating wreck I'd ever left him, but it was worth more because he thought it was safe from my retribution.

~~~~~~

It was 7:00 a.m. by the time I returned the keys to Sergiu's phone drawer and parked the Pinto in front of Tricia's house. I had gone from one end of Dallas to the other and then back again. I was deliriously tired. I did not want to deal with Sergiu, but he was standing in the living room waiting.

"Constanzia," he drew the syllables out long. "Where you go?"

The house was small and there were not a lot of places to retreat. I didn't want to enter my room because he'd follow, and I didn't much care for what happened in there. The kitchen was too close to Tricia's room, and besides not wanting to wake her, I didn't want to draw her into whatever this was about to become. So I remained just inside the door, putting on my innocent face to say, "Out for a drive."

"Constanzia," it was full of warning. "You make me angry?"

I could not stop a smirk from turning my face evil.

132

"You go to my house?"

Laughter rolled in my throat with pleasure.

"You use knife in my closet?"

I let him wonder for a few moments before reminding him, "You know I prefer your cars."

He looked pleased and asked, "You like car in garage?"

"Yes, actually." I was softly laughing, but he was confused.

"There is no car in garage."

"Well," I conceded, "not in *your* garage."

He had a little think about that, and then shook his head to deny his thoughts were possible. "You smart girl, but no so smart to find my car."

Not smart enough to find a car with a parking receipt? I didn't want to give away the surprise, but I also couldn't stand to have my intelligence insulted. I was smug, "The Aston Martin won't be going to New York."

This made him quiet. He was searching his head for the meaning of my words, and then understanding slowly spread across his face with a smile. He was only able to ask, "Constanzia?" Then he had to take a moment, curling his finger over his lips so he wouldn't break into a laugh. Somewhat composed but too amused, he asked, "You?" and punched a fist into his open palm. "You do this with Aston Martin?"

"Did you not think I would find it?"

He caught a laugh, asked, "Constanzia?" Another laugh, "You think I have Aston Martin?" Then disbelief, "This car is hundred thousand dollars." He inclined his head with appreciation, "Maybe half million if you," hand punch, "a special car."

I stopped breathing.

The smile was sliding off my face.

It wasn't his.

But it was a hundred thousand maybe half a million dollars.

Going a little dizzy, I inhaled too deeply, closed my eyes and covered my face.

There was only one explanation for it. Sergiu's cologne smelled cold in the car because I reeked of it. I was the one who made the car smell of Givenchy, and I'd left it to cool while searching for another car with unlocked doors.

I dropped my head with sickening dread, murmuring to myself, "Oh, no, no. No. No. No."

And Sergiu was chuckling, "Is okay. I fix this. You tell me, where is car?"

"No, no, no." I had not just destroyed some unknown person's very expensive car.

"Is no problem, Constanzia." Sergiu gripped me by the shoulder. "I fix. Tell me where is car."

I'd wiped clean the door, steering wheel, black box, and gear shift, but not the tarp. I didn't know if the police could get fingerprints off the tarp. And then it occurred to me, I'd touched everything in the glove compartment. "Oh, this is bad." I did not want to explain to Rick, or any of the authorities associated with my case, why I had gone into a parking garage and shredded the exterior of a stranger's

Aston Martin. There was just no excuse for that. I would be sent back to the psych ward. "Very bad."

"Constanzia," Sergiu was calm now, trying to placate.

And I was nearly accusing, "It had a push button start. Why would it have a push button start? It didn't need a key."

"Is probably stolen."

"Ohhoho," the word shuddered out and I was bending at the waist to expel the hysteria. "Stolen. Oh, God. That is lovely." Now I was going to be charged with stealing *and* destroying a hundred thousand maybe half a million dollar car. It appeared I was going to have a prison experience as well.

Sergiu had me by the back of the neck, drawing me up to look at him. He was no longer amused but serious, "Where is car?"

Yes, exactly. I had to get back to the car. Immediately.

Whirling around for the door, "I have to go."

Then Sergiu had me by my shoulders, pulling me back, complaining to the Madonna in Italian, but I was ducking free, opening the door. He caught me around the waist, kicked the door closed, and swung me back into the room.

I was adamant, voice rising, "I have no time for this now," and he was carrying on in broken English and another language, but I wasn't listening. I was struggling to get loose, insisting in a variety of combinations, "I've been moronic. I am going to be arrested. Let me go," not hearing a thing he said until he squeezed me so hard I squeaked to breathe.

"You calm?"

"Yes."

"I fix. Where is car?"

I was angry. "I don't need you to *fix*. It's a simple ..." then I was squeezed to squeaking silence again.

"You no so good with this. I fix. This is my job. Where is car?"

If I told him where it was, he would know I had found his receipts. And while he probably didn't share my sentiment that going through his private effects was a greater offense than destroying the cars, he'd still hide those effects, preventing me from finding the cars, even if I hadn't actually found one. Shit was a mess.

"Constanzia, you make this hard for me. You tell me now, I fix now. It is late. There will be people."

Argh, I was growling. He was making me feel guilty when really, "This is as much your fault as mine."

"Is my fault. Yes. Where is car?"

I couldn't bring myself to speak. I hated yielding, but he wasn't letting go.

"I am sorry. Is my fault. I fix. You tell me, where is car?" And when he didn't get an answer, he clinched his arms tight again, asking, "*Tell me?*" and then tighter until I was making breathless sounds of agreement.

He didn't relent until he had the address of the garage, knew the car was under a tarp on the third level, and that my fingerprints were in the glove box. Then he hugged me hard, kissed me on the cheek and left cheerful, telling me, "I bring you something from New York."

~~~~~

136

My head was being undone by a powerful swell of gratitude that felt like it was rising from my heart, thankful Sergiu was going to clean up my mess. And the way he had said, "I fix. This is my job," was reassuring. He was going to protect me from my idiotic act, and that he even cared enough to risk himself made me grateful.

But I was shaking tired and capable of twisting my thoughts into all manner of perverse logic, and very little of it was reasoned out by the time he returned.

He and Daniel arrived in a loud flurry of activity, hauling in bags of groceries and wines, calling for me and Tricia to join them; and for the first time in months, I wanted to, but I judged the desire as a betrayal against myself and rather pathetic in its need. I hated that I even thought it, but I wished it could all go back to the way it had once been, when I could shamelessly enjoy Sergiu's company. But instead, I was guarding against any further drop in my resolve, having to remind myself that Sergiu was not a friend.

He was in my room, encouraging me to accept a present from New York, saying, "You will like," and then pressing, "Open."

The box said Bvlgari again, and holding it in my hand, I suspected it was earrings. My curiosity to see them was high, but the offering made me feel exactly like a whore. I wanted to turn the scene confrontational, to ask Sergiu if he was trying to buy my emotions or my forgiveness, but I couldn't bring myself to speak when I knew it was little more than payment for sex.

I was disturbed enough for feeling indebted over the Aston Martin; I wasn't going to willingly bankrupt my wavering self-respect for jewelry. I slipped the box wordlessly into his jacket pocket while shaking my head no, and Sergiu dipped his head in concession.

At first I thought he understood, but then he said, "Is okay. I keep. You will take it later."

The assumption should have earned him a contemptuous laugh, but I couldn't raise my amusement high enough for condescension.

He pulled me into a hard embrace, saying, "You make it hard for me, but is good, I like," and then when I pushed back, he clamped onto my shoulder to direct me into the kitchen, saying with great delight, "I show you how to cook cappellone."

The spread across the counters meant he and Daniel planned to cook through the afternoon, and Sergiu was determined I was going to stay. He kept passing me things to do, instructing, "You open bottle," or, "Read the directions," and then when I moved to leave, he'd step me back to the table, insisting, "I no understand this, read again," and all because of the Aston Martin, I felt obligated to comply.

The whole incident kept me self-conscious, and Sergiu knew it. From his arrival, he had been watching me, waiting, wanting me to ask if he had taken care of my mistake. I imagined he planned to blow it off with, "Of course," and then hold me at fault for questioning his word, as though I had no right or reason; and I didn't need him messing with my head when I was doing a fine enough job on my own.

138

Daniel was at the counter just starting to chop up onions, and by the way he kept looking at me, I could tell that he knew, but I doubted he had been told why I continued to feel the need to destroy expensive cars. Imagining I had been labeled as the-crazy-jealous-type just added to my tension.

Trying to get me to smile, Sergiu was telling a story that had happened in New York. "I go to see old woman in hospital. She no so good. Maybe she no stay long," he turned his hand to show it was iffy. "I know her very little but she mother of friend, so I must go. But I no want to go alone, so I take Daniel and Eugene. *Uf*," Sergiu rolled his eyes at what had obviously been a mistake, and Daniel laughed guiltily over the cutting board.

"I take her big bouquet of flowers, you know?"

He made a large circle with his hands to indicate its size, and I nodded that I understood.

"This woman is very … ah … popular. She have many bouquets," and his hands spread up the wall to indicate they were stacked high and wide in the room. "My friend is there and we talk. I think his mother is asleep, so we very close, *shhh*, talking quiet. But behind me," he waved his fingers over his shoulder, "I see Eugene …" and then he lightly jabbed a finger erratically in a small circle before his face, "counting. He is in the bouquets counting. I think, 'Perdinci, he make trouble.' The Româns no like …" He looked to me for the word, "Two, four, six, eight, what is this?"

"Even numbers?"

"Yes, the Româns no like even numbers with flowers. Eugene think we curse the old woman. He think we leave these flowers, she die, so he counting all the bouquets, pulling out the flower that make it even."

Daniel's shoulders were shaking over the cutting board, and little gasps of humor were choking him.

"He have many flowers in hand when I see him, and I no want trouble, so I keep my friend looking this way," Sergiu pointed forward, "but I waving back here," behind his back, "for Daniel to stop Eugene."

Daniel was heaving laughter now, trying to pant out something in Romanian.

Sergiu listened and then confirmed, "Yes, Eugene hit in head too many time with ball. He good tennis player, but the ball up here," he pointed at his skull, "it no make it over net."

"He playing on empty court," Daniel concurred.

"I think my friend's mother is asleep, but no, she is watching Eugene. She is angry. She say to Eugene, 'Are you the gardener or you forget flowers for date?' *Ahi*!" Sergiu threw his hands up in surprise. "Now my friend see and he is angry. He want Eugene to leave but Eugene have many flowers in hand. It is like he make a new bouquet. The problem is, this new bouquet is also even, so Eugene no give it back. But my friend want flowers. I tell Eugene to give but he ..." Sergiu wrestled with an imaginary cluster of flowers to rip one free, "he take one." Sergiu shook his head, and Daniel was bent at the waist laughing. "But my friend, he want this flower, too."

"The flower is no pretty," Daniel explained.

"No," Sergiu agreed. "Eugene take flower and ..." he twisted his hands like he were wringing a dishtowel. "But no matter, my friend he want. Is mother's flower. I speak angry with Eugene in romaneste," and to accentuate it, Sergiu clamped his hand on my shoulder. "He understand I am serious and he give me flower. I give flower to my friend with many apologies, but my friend take flower and return it to bouquet in hand." Sergiu closed his eyes and shook his head to deny the next memory while Daniel wheezed for breath. "Eugene …" and then a string of Italian that I assumed meant *that-son-of-a-bitch*, "he make crazy tennis feet to take flower back," and Sergiu plucked it out of the air. "Now I have to hit him," and by the demonstration, it was apparently upside the head with an open palm. "And the flower is …" by his pained expression, it was gruesomely mangled.

The story had done what Sergiu intended. I was smiling to imagine it, and he was pleased with himself for making me to laugh.

Chuckling with me, he remembered, "There is wedding soon." The thought of Eugene ravaging the floral arrangements at a church had both Daniel and I laughing, but Sergiu assured us, "I no take Eugene to wedding."

~~~~~~

Sergiu would often recount events from New York, but he never talked about what he did, or who he worked for. I knew the cars were stolen because it was obvious, and I knew essentially, though not exactly, who he worked for because he had told me his name and the reason he'd left Italy. I wondered when he said it if he knew his surname had been in *Time* magazine. If he didn't, I wasn't going to be the one to tell him. I was pretending I had never heard it, or of it.

But it was part of the exciting world I thought was passing me by in small-town Shelbyville. Even so, I couldn't quite remember why I thought it when I was in his presence. Day-to-day existence was still largely boring. About the only thing truly exhilarating was driving fast and doing donuts into dumpsters. That just never seemed to get old.

But I was pretty tired of what led to it. I didn't know how long it could go on before he learned it wasn't worth it.

He had come to the house in a Mercedes, a big hulking black sedan that I thought was a little too luxurious for him to risk, so I had relaxed as the afternoon turned into evening, and I was laughing with him over dinner.

I expected him to leave, but then he was in my room saying, "I stay with you tonight."

I thought we had established the Pinto was code for sex.

I looked out the window at the Mercedes and warned, "Are you sure? It could get expensive."

He was very plain, "You take car again, I hurt you."

The rush of blood to my face was an unfamiliar shock. His emotionless tone scared me more than anger.

Still, it took a moment for me to decide. He was threatening an escalation. Black eyes or broken bones, whichever, he planned to hit me. And I knew he'd do it. And I didn't want to be hurt. And besides, I convinced myself, after decimating six cars, I wasn't really winning. I didn't need Sergiu to knock the smirk off my face because the Aston

142

Martin had already done it. But then my smile had already been fading. In the past month, I'd had a hard time finding any amusement with the Dallas experience. It had become a bit of a chore. And if I wasn't going to dismantle his car as a consequence, there wasn't much point in fighting Sergiu either.

I was battling myself now and quietly submitting was devastating. Nothing in Dallas had managed to bring me to the edge of tears, but letting him use my body without struggle was awful, and I was crying.

He said, "You relax. You safe with me. I let no one hurt you."

I couldn't think of anyone that wanted to hurt me except, "You … you're the one …"

"*Shhh*, no, I good with you. I no hurt you. I let you break six cars. Yes?"

Well, yes, and I suppose I should be thankful; no, wait, something wasn't right with that. "You … I only …" but I was crying and couldn't speak.

"You take car again, I hurt you, but I no break what I keep. You, I teach. You learn slow, but is okay, I patient."

I was thankful he didn't have full command of English because that was a psychotic masterpiece of intimidation. I didn't know whether to be grateful or terrified, but I knew I was being played by a master. I could appreciate the art of his manipulation, and I fully recognized what he was doing, but the knowledge didn't prevent my emotions from being exploited.

The last resistance I could maintain was a refusal to speak our real names.

"I want to hear you say my name."

I shook my head.

"Say my name. Say Marco."

"Sergiu."

"You tell me your name," but no matter how hard he gripped my throat or ripped at my hair, the only name I would give in return was Constance.

Death Threats

Ron Howard's assistants were getting suspicious. They had not once spoken to me or even heard my voice in the background. They would press Tricia to put me on the phone, but I would have fled the house. They didn't know if I was even aware a deal was being negotiated. They called Rick.

But I was backing away from that phone call too. I didn't want to explain to Rick that I couldn't see him. There was no way I could explain Sergiu or his threat, and no other excuse would make sense.

It was best to just ignore everything and hope it worked itself out.

The strategy seemed to be working until I returned from the park to hear Tricia say, "Rick will be here in an hour."

Oh, no, no. I called his apartment but he was already gone.

I dropped my head and covered my eyes to think. I used to always say, "I can handle it. I've handled worse," but I was no longer so certain of the first, and Dallas just kept delivering the worst.

It didn't have to spin out of control though. Daniel was in the house and that was bad, but Sergiu was on his way to New York. If I got rid of Rick quickly, by the time Sergiu returned, the visit might have been so inconsequential, it wouldn't be mentioned.

When Rick arrived, I was sitting on the porch reading a book and greeted him with an unfriendly expression, as though I were annoyed to be disturbed.

He explained he hadn't seen me in well over a month, and because I was no longer at the refugee agency, it was difficult to reach me by phone.

I didn't lift my face from the page but muttered, "I'm fine."

He became concerned when the Hollywood assistants called him with suggestions I might not actually be living with Tricia.

Turning the page, "I'm here. I simply have nothing to say."

He was trying, but I was cold and aloof, and when he stayed, I turned nearly hostile eyes on him, questioning why he remained.

"Well, I just wanted to make sure you were okay."

"Fine, thank you." The goodbye was implicit when I dropped my attention back to the book.

I'd been extraordinarily impolite and felt horrible. And just as bad, I couldn't think of a reason Rick would continue to help me if this was the gratitude he got.

I was never going to get identification under Sergiu's conditions, which meant I couldn't work or move on.

But I'd staved off a horrible scene for a while. I didn't know if Sergiu would really try to kill Rick, but I felt certain there would be a confrontation, or some sort of berserk incident I would be asked to explain.

I wanted desperately to avoid that, so I'd been disgracefully rude.

But I hadn't gotten in the vehicle with Rick. I hadn't left. The exchange was brief. I was confident disaster had been averted.

By the time Sergiu returned, I had honestly forgotten about it.

Daniel knew he was coming and invited Tricia to join him for an evening ride. I was clueless.

I was sitting on the floor reading the newspaper when he came through the front door, and by his expression, I knew remaining so low would be hazardous. I got to my feet in case I had to flee. It was by far the angriest I'd ever seen him. He'd never hit me before — he'd choked me, flung me about, and wrung my hair — but he'd never actually hauled off and struck me, and I was afraid he was about to.

Hands out in treaty, I was saying, "Wait, wait, wait, I don't know why you're mad."

"I tell you, you see him again, I kill him."

"I didn't."

"You did." He seemed particularly huge with his temper uncontrolled, and the room had always been too small for him.

He was standing in line with all three exits and I had a wall at my back. I tried to reason, saying with soft calm, "There has been a misunderstanding."

He stepped forward and I stepped back, continuing, "You have no reason to be angry."

He moved forward again but another step back would have me against the wall and I didn't want to be pinned. I couldn't edge right or left without coming into his reach, and now my voice lost its calm. "I've given you no cause."

But he kept coming, so I stamped my foot and declared, "You have no right."

"I tell you, I kill him," and then abruptly, he was turning with all his fury to leave.

I said flatly, "Wait. Just wait. You need to see something," then called him to follow me into my room. "I know who you've been working for," and from my bedside drawer I flipped out his phone bill with the calls to New York and their numbers listed in the tolls. "You touch Rick and I swear, I'll rip every one of you apart so savagely, you'll think what I did to the cars was a mother's kiss."

He was staggered and swayed with the threat. Eyes large, he recovered to consider my confrontational stare with shock and trepidation. He was taking it all in, what I had said, how I'd gotten the phone bill, why I even had it, and what it revealed.

He moved forward to take it, his hand open wide in a display he wasn't going to hurt me, concerned I might back away from him again, but I stepped up to meet him, extending it, saying, "I don't need it. It's all on record."

Slowly, he began to turn his head and wag his finger with warning, "You, no. This," taking the phone bill to crumple it, "very bad."

"I know."

"This make much trouble."

I smiled in agreement.

"You no understand what you say."

"Not only do I understand, I see you understand as well."

"Constanzia …"

"Sergiu."

The last insult was too much. He threw his hand up to show we were through and left.

~~~~~~

For the next three days, I called Rick's apartment and hung up when I confirmed he was alive. I had done it again right after Sergiu arrived with bags of food and wine.

He'd spent most of the day cooking with Daniel and aggressively not acknowledging me.

It was early evening and the meal was nearly ready when he finally pulled me toward the front door saying, "Come, we talk."

But instead of speaking, we walked silently into the park, farther onto the golf course, and then, beneath a line of trees, he stopped and I turned to look at him. From his jacket pocket, he pulled out a revolver, held it to my head and pulled the trigger.

I said, "That's not funny."

He pulled the trigger again.

I knocked his arm away, saying, "Seriously, don't play like that with guns," but he grabbed me by the neck and put the pistol back against my temple to pull the trigger three more times in rapid succession.

Now I was pissed, saying, "You're going to blow my damn head off."

But he was confused. He frowned while opening the cylinder and dumping the empty cartridges into his palm.

I demanded his attention, asking, "Are you unaware of how many deaths occur when people fool around like this?"

He held his hand up for patience while he looked through his pockets. He pulled the change from one side of his pants and inspected it, holding a finger up for me to wait, then felt around his other before turning to his jacket pockets, and all the while I was angrily watching him. Finally, from inside his jacket, he found a bullet. He raised his hand for just a moment's more tolerance while he loaded the gun.

I was stamping off for the house when he grabbed me by the shoulder. Trying to shrug him off, I snapped, "Marco, I am not going to play Russian Roulette with you."

Then I was walking free and heard from behind, "You say my name."

"It was an accident."

He growled, caught up, and jerked me around. He wanted to say something but he was angry and confused, hopeful and exasperated, his features contorting as each emotion gave way to the next; and every time he opened his mouth to speak, one hand marked each painful change with a sharp gesture, while in the other, the pistol was held at his side.

And I was staring with irritation.

His frustration punched him in the stomach, bending him at the waist, making him bellow. He rose up to yell at me, "You make much trouble for me!"

"Good," I was glad to hear it.

Hands clamped to his head, the gun was pressed flat against his temple and he was demanding, "You crazy?"

"At this point, yes, I think a little."

He dropped his hands and then his shoulders followed in defeat. Shaking his head to dispel his thoughts, he returned the revolver to his pocket and said with resignation, "We go eat now."

~~~~~~

On about the third day, it finally registered with me what had happened on the golf course. It was one of those harsh realizations where your head swivels because something that should have been plainly obvious gets knocked across your face like a steel bat.

I thought, "He tried to kill me."

I wasn't terribly surprised, or even upset, I was just tired. I couldn't think of a reason to continue with the elaborate fiction I was playing. At some point it had gone horribly wrong, and I was looking at a place very close to the beginning. It had to do with sex, and everyone asking me who I'd had it with. And it was sex right up to the end that was causing so much grief.

I didn't want to go forward and I didn't want to go back. Both options seemed like a hassle. I was sitting on the couch, absently wondering what it would be like to swallow a family-sized bottle of aspirin. I'd heard it was a painful way to go, but once the aspirin made it into your system, there was nothing a medical team could do to save you. It was permanent, which at least guaranteed I wouldn't be returned to the mental hospital.

My thoughts must have been on my face because Tricia stopped as she passed through the living room. She dropped into the corner of the couch to sit crooked and study me. I knew she was concerned, but I didn't have enough energy to fake a smile. She said, "Why don't you tell me where you're from."

I didn't look at her but answered, "Tennessee."

She was quiet for a long time before asking, "Your story isn't true, is it?"

"Not a bit of it."

"How old are you?"

"Fifteen."

I heard her breath stop. Even louder, I heard her draw her next breath in. She asked, "Did you say fifteen?"

"Yes."

"Is that the truth?"

"Yes."

She sat back. After a moment, she shared what she'd been thinking. "It all makes sense now. You think like a teenager. You don't look like one, but you make decisions like a teenager. Did you know I have a daughter that's sixteen?"

I turned to face her.

"She lives with her father. She doesn't really like me, but she's at that age." Then she asked, "Do you have a mother?"

"Yes."

"Do you love her?"

"Yes."

"I love my daughter, too. If my daughter were missing, I know what I'd be going through. I couldn't live with myself if I didn't make you call your mother."

I nodded.

She handed me the phone, reinforcing, "You have to call your parents."

It was my father that answered. I said, "Hi Dad, it's me."

"Tanya?"

"Yes."

"Where are you?"

"Dallas."

He said, "I love you." I knew he did. I'd heard it countless times before, but this time it made me cry. He was calm though. He had it all under control. He said, "There will be a ticket waiting for you at the airport counter. Go and get it now."

So I went home and told my parents what I had been doing for the past seven months, telling them about the FBI and Interpol and the mental institution, Congress and the ACLU and Ron Howard. Then I heard my father on the phone with the hospital, saying, "I think she's been doing drugs."

It was the only way to account for the mad story I was telling.

But he came back and started to ask specifics, and eventually stuck on the name Rick with the Collin County Sheriff's Department. He called the detective, and Rick told him that Ron Howard and the ACLU and Interpol were all ringing, wanting to know where I was, but worst among them was Ron Howard's assistants who wanted to know what the hell was going on.

I heard my father explaining who I was and where I was, and then the funniest exchange occurred.

Rick must have asked, "How old is she?"

Because my father started answering, "Fifteen," and then again, "Fifteen," and when Rick didn't think that was right, my father continued to confirm, "No, she's fifteen ... One, five ... Fifteen ... No, you're not hearing wrong, she's fifteen ... Fifteen ... Detective, I know how old my daughter is ... Alright: one-two-three-four-five-six-seven-eight-nine-ten-eleven-twelve, thirteen, fourteen, *fifteen*." Then a longer pause while he listened and responded with solace, "It's alright son, I understand, she's very charming."

THE AFTERMATH

The headlines across the country started much the same: "Authorities Fooled by Teen," or "Teenager Tricked Officials," and also "Authorities Duped by Runaway," but they all essentially printed in bold: "Girl Fooled Officials with White Slavery Tale."

The opening paragraphs were nearly identical as well:

A 15-year-old girl who ran away from her Tennessee home fooled authorities for seven months with tales of an international white slavery ring before she finally gave up the masquerade.

Of all the agencies that investigated and examined her – the Collin County Sheriff's Department, Wichita Falls State Hospital, the FBI, the Immigration and Naturalization Service, the Drug Enforcement Administration and Interpol – none could find a flaw in her story.

There's a massive difference in not finding a flaw and being fooled. The problem with the headlines was very few people were genuinely deceived; they just didn't know what to do with me. I stuck to my story and didn't make many mistakes, and the ones I did, people were willing to overlook or forget.

But still the papers asked: *How did she fool all those investigators for all those months?*

I'm quoted as saying, "Creative genius."

Rick confirmed that and then said, "I was dealing with a mastermind."

He went on to say, "It wouldn't have surprised me if she had known half the things I was thinking."

And then, "It's the most bizarre thing this office has ever encountered. I'm not angered because it's very logical ... a person with the IQ she has could easily have pulled this off. And she did."

It might have been easy but it wasn't logical. I also think he might have been cut off and that was meant to read, "It's very logical that someone with her IQ would get bored and think it entertaining to cut loose all the cannons on a ship."

He did say, "Despite the testing in Wichita Falls, Tanya needs 'psychological services of some kind.'"

That assessment was going to be shared by many, but it was a tiny sentence that didn't make it into many papers. The big story was that a 15-year-old had told an elaborate tale of white slavery, and the Texas authorities had been duped.

But that wasn't accurate. I caused a lot of doubt in everyone's mind, and not even Sergiu suspected I was so young, or American. But the only person I fooled, full out, from start to finish, was the deputy in Shelbyville who had helped me run away.

Now that poor man, I had truly tricked. Our short encounter had been a fast, hard con, and that's where I truly excelled.

~~~~~~

With some hope of trying to make sense of what I'd done, the local psychologist gave me the Stanford–Binet Intelligence test. She looked worried with the results. At 176, I was just a few points higher

156

than the test actually allowed, and she'd had to calculate the score separately.

It didn't make her nearly as happy to tell me this as it did for me to hear it.

She tried for a better result with the Wechsler Intelligence test. The Wechsler version gave no extra points for answering with speed, and I'd racked up fourteen points for going fast, but the difference wasn't enough to provide her any comfort.

In my case, intelligence was a disease that had led to a psychotic episode. But I had returned home of my own will and freely admitted my behavior while away, so it was diagnosed as nothing more than that, an episode.

Hoping to prevent my madness from resurfacing, the psychologist spoke with the dean of the nearby community college and convinced him to accept me into the school based on the scores.

After two tests, one interview, and admission into college, the psychologist didn't think there was much more she could offer. She warned my parents I would likely do something again if I was not mentally challenged, but, "Other than a high need for stimulation, Tanya is mentally healthy."

I quoted the first news article, "Either that or 'a deeply disturbed, very capable liar.'"

But no one in the room found that funny. It was a little too close to what everyone suspected.

My humor hadn't changed and I felt much the same, but I was viewed differently. I was an unsettling presence in the community that caused people to fall silent. Strangers and friends had to step back for a bit of perspective. They needed to quietly inspect me for cracks, afraid I might break mental at any moment.

One woman was bold enough to ask, "Are you better now?"

I had no idea how to answer that, and it really didn't matter because nothing I said would make people comfortable with me again. There were questions they couldn't ask and I couldn't guess. The papers said slave, but they didn't mention sex, and the connection was clear to everyone except me.

My father was very disturbed. He no longer believed my behavior with older men had been entirely innocent, and I wasn't going to tell him that it wasn't, and neither was I.

But that was something everybody needed to be protected from. It was an image my parents did not need in their head. After every other heartache I had caused them over the past seven months, I did not want my mother crying while my father drove to Texas with a gun.

He was worried enough without knowing about Sergiu, and already he felt the need to express the importance of men respecting women. I agreed. Time and again, I agreed, but he had three dozen ways to say it and a long summer to say it in.

He finally got around to saying, "I never spanked you."

"And I appreciate it."

"And I never let that school touch you either."

The high school had corporal punishment and had tried, but I'd refused to submit. It turned into a three-hour battle with four teachers and the principal. By midafternoon, the principal threatened to call my father and I begged, "Please do."

They were quickly familiarized with what happens when you stand between a protective father and his youngest child. He was furious, demanding of the administration, "I don't hit my daughter, so what makes you think I'm going to permit you?" In half the time it took to drive there, he was in the office, and then everyone was hiding their wooden paddles lest he follow through with his threat to try it out on them first.

Why he felt the need to remind me was a mystery, and he'd only say, "No one over the age of four needs to be spanked."

I said, "Okay. But I told you when I was five I was never having kids, and I haven't changed my mind."

"I'm not worried about you having kids."

I couldn't imagine who else he thought I might hit. The lesson was making less and less sense. Maybe he thought I had quintessentially changed. I tried to reassure him, "I'm not violent. I'd never hurt anyone."

That admission made nothing better. He shook his head and asked, "You know Star?" Star was his best friend's daughter. She had five PhD's by the time she was 30 and a black belt in karate when she was 12. She was a 13-year-old senior when the six-foot captain of the basketball team passed her in the hall and grabbed her breast. She bounced him down the hall, knocking him off one locker after the next, never letting him fully regain his feet, slamming him one direction to break his nose, and then hurling him another to blacken his eyes. Before she was done making an example of him, she'd cracked his wrist and a rib. After a two-week suspension, she came back to part the crowded halls like Moses at the sea. My father said, "Star never took any shit. You could learn a lot from Star."

Paper Hanging

My parents cautiously waited for me to turn sixteen so I could drive myself to college, but I'd waited for the driver's license so I could continue my search for legitimate identification under an assumed name. I kept Sergiu's secrets, mentioning him only as the person who had taught me to drive. When I failed the road test, no one was too impressed with his tutoring, but by the fall semester, I'd managed to stop slinging the testing official into the passenger window on the corners, and finally passed when I recognized the stop signs and speed limits weren't just friendly suggestions.

Having procured my first piece of genuine identification, I understood the basic exchange of information required to get another. You needed something easy like a library card, school form, or bank book, and then a birth certificate.

I was fortunate to have been born at the cusp of all things bad. My birth did not require an immediate Social Security number to see the doctor. My parents only applied for it when I was twelve so I could open a saving's account. Social Security hadn't yet turned into our official identity number, so I didn't have to offer it to get my first driver's license.

The problem was the birth certificate. I studied mine, which had been issued in New York, and my sister's issued in Miami. I looked at my friends' birth certificates from Los Angeles, Atlanta, and Nashville, and then all the small towns of Tennessee. Every one of them was different and most of them were laughably plain without raised seals, official stamps, or even a watermark for security. I was convinced there was no way the Tennessee Department of Driver's License Services was confirming these shoddy typewriter-abused pieces of paper were genuine. I knew I could forge them if I could get access to a laser printer. But at the time, laser printers cost four thousand dollars, and even my professors only had access to dot matrix.

I needed a laser printer and an IBM computer.

But then I had another idea. I went back to the license center and said, "I lost my driver's license."

They said, "Well, you'll need to get your picture taken again to make a new one."

I asked, "Don't you have a copy of my picture on file?"

"No, we don't make copies."

Oh man, oh-man-oh-man, there was a question I wanted to ask but didn't know how to phrase. I worked and worked for a way to say it without giving away my intentions, but there was no subtle way to ask, "So, you're just taking my word that I am the person on the license?" I went ahead and asked it.

"You *are* aged sixteen, five-foot-eight with brown hair and eyes," like duh, it's your description you idiotic little girl.

"And the only place this picture exists is on my license?"

"It's the only place it needs to exist."

I didn't believe her. There was no way it was that simple. I went to another licensing center to have the same conversation a second time, and then I went slightly giddy with wonder.

I had the local printers run a thousand stylish flyers and then plastered them all over Nashville and Atlanta.

Models needed for winter runway work. Must be over eighteen and between 5'8" and 5'9". Headshots preferred but photographs accepted. Please send details to: P.O. Box in Nashville.

The Caucasian models with brown, black, or red hair received a phone call.

"This all sounds excellent. I think you'll be *perfect* for the team. You'll absolutely *love* the other nine girls. I need to send you a contract, but before I do, I just need proof you're over eighteen. If you could mail to the same P.O. Box a copy of your driver's license or birth certificate, either will be fine, both would be even better. And you know what? Just throw in your Social Security number while you're at it — you know how the auditors are with taxes these days," and we'd both groan at the trouble they caused.

It hadn't been intended, but I ended up with nearly twenty original or certified birth certificates. It was 1986 and identity fraud was not yet a publicized issue, and, as I discovered, models were absolutely desperate to please. It made them terribly easy to manipulate, a trait that simultaneously pleased and distressed me. They needed to be protected from the likes of me, but I knew there were people with intentions far worse than mine that would cause them no end of unhappiness.

By the end of our chatty conversations, I knew their mother's maiden name, what their father did for a living, and where everyone in their family was born. I'd put the phone down knowing every distinct detail of their identity so that I didn't really need a copy of anything, but I still asked for them to send it.

Almost always I walked away disturbed by the hope and expectation I was going to shatter. My greatest concern was the weeks of anxiety I would cause when they didn't get the promised contract. I could imagine it, and I couldn't stomach it. I sent them all apology letters explaining the show had been canceled but I would keep their details for the spring event.

Conscience appeased, I organized the treasure into a file. Some names were only copies of the driver's license, most came with Social Security numbers, and almost twenty had genuine birth certificates.

I started going to the Driver's Licensing Service Centers and saying, "Hi, I'm Ms. Model and I lost my license. That's me alright: aged twenty, five-foot-eight with brown hair and eyes."

~~~~~~

Every week I added another Tennessee issued driver's license to my collection. The names and addresses were unfamiliar but the picture in the corner was clearly me. In some my hair was flaming red, and in others I was Goth, but the high cheek bones and strong lines of my face remained the same. I was never going to be a spy that could don a disguise and meld into any person. But as Tennessee didn't keep a copy of the pictures on file, the risks associated with my crime were so low as to be nonexistent.

There was nothing to slow me down, and I wasn't going to stop until I had at least a dozen IDs, and a few more from Georgia, but I had very little idea of what I wanted to do with them.

For inspiration, I went to the library to look up con artists and fraud. The books repeatedly referenced check kiting. If it hadn't had such an appealing name, I might have overlooked it, but I just loved saying the words: check kiting.

It sounded breezy, but essentially it was nothing more than writing one bad check to cover another. It's illegal the very moment you don't have the funds to cover either check, but it becomes particularly criminal when you withdraw the erroneous balance that's been created.

History's most outrageous kiters had brought several major banks to their knees, and because of it, the banks were on the lookout for similar activity. But as the library books explained, it was more difficult to spot by using multiple accounts with different names. The more accounts, the longer you could float the checks.

There was no risk I would bankrupt a bank when all I needed was five thousand dollars. The goal was a laser printer and a computer so I could continue my experiments in creating legal identification.

I opened four checking accounts in four unique names at four separate banks in four adjoining states, and then I started writing checks from one account to the other, keeping them all up in the air, in transit, increasing the value of deposits until I had withdrawn nearly eight thousand dollars. Then I let the checks fall where they may, and whose ever name was on the license got to explain they hadn't been involved.

When I had opened the accounts, each bank had taken photocopies of the driver's license with my image in the corner, and while the pictures were black blobs of grainy ink, barely recognizable as female, I assumed it was enough to clear the models of wrong doing. The fear that I would mess up anyone's life didn't prevent me from doing it, but it did keep me from continuing the practice.

Not wanting to explain to my parents how I came to be in possession of the computer and printing equipment, I kept it at a friend's house. John Mittwede and I had classes together three times a week. Every Monday, Wednesday, and Friday, we'd leave campus to race each other through the curvy back roads to his house. I had a six-cylinder Mustang and no fear of passing on the curves, so it was a race he never won. Early on he declared me crazy and himself foolish for playing games with a lunatic.

When he met my grandmother, he thought she was prophetic because she could never get his name right, always calling him Nitwitty.

"And I am a nitwit for letting you do this here." From the very start, he protested, but he was also an artist, and he found immense joy in the new technology of laser printing. He wanted to see what the printer could do, but not in the same way I did.

"There are better things to use this for than birth certificates," but then he'd grimace and criticize that I was doing it wrong, without style and with no regard for perfection.

I'd say, "They won't notice," and wave it away, but he couldn't bear to see it.

He'd smoke a joint, eat some pills, and then shoo me away from the computer to do it himself. When I pulled the documents from the printer to finish them, I was reminded he didn't like my handwriting either. I could forge a signature better than he, but as long as we were making everybody up out of air and imagination, he thought the mother's and father's signatures should complement the doctor's. The husband's should be dark and bold, the wife's should scroll fancifully across the paper, and the doctor had to dominate them both with decisive authority, then everybody had to have the proper amount of loops both above and below the line.

I would laugh at his obsession, but his need for visual harmony meant he made all of the birth certificates I used, and he made them very pretty. The agents at the Driver's License Service Centers never remarked on this however. They just took the document for how it appeared and started me with the written exam. This I never failed, but I'd still roll through the stop signs, pass in the intersections, or think the agent would just love to read the book on the backseat and reach around to get it, then I'd have to return to take the road test again.

~~~~~~

Check kiting was more amusing to say than do, but it gave me a taste for banks. I liked the feel of banks. I liked the ones with marble floors and chandeliers as much as the ones with corporate carpet and stained paneling. I was comfortable in the hushed atmosphere that was so similar to a library. I not only liked the little slips of paper you had to fill out to deposit or withdraw, but also the black pens on ball chains that would loop so nicely into a circle. I adored the antique vaults and was mesmerized by the rows of safety deposit boxes. I imagined they held fabulous secrets. The women wore dresses and the men wore suits, and everything was so very tidy. Banks were marvelous.

And I could be twenty-three again. It was a good age to acquire a loan. I asked for five-thousand dollars, and all the loan officers wanted in return was a copy of a 1040 tax return and proof of employment. It didn't seem right that it should be so easy.

I expected to be caught by some unexpected security feature. I thought I was wasting money renting a house, setting up a phone, and then waiting for the bank to call so I could confirm I worked at whatever imaginary business I had named on the form.

I wondered if I really could just get away with filling out a 1040EZ and then photocopying it, as though this alone were evidence of filing with the IRS, but it never failed to appease.

It was harder to get a Social Security number than five thousand dollars.

But not much harder.

I entered the banks looking civil, but I would go into Social Security like a backwoods holy-roller. With my hair brushed straight and rolled into a bun, I finished the look of a Pentecostal by scrubbing my face clean of makeup and wearing socks in sandals under a long floral skirt. The clothes I wore had been homemade and were well-used by the time I bought them at the Salvation Army, so no one doubted that if it were Sunday, I'd be speaking in tongues or proselytizing with snakes; but as it was midweek, I was staring at the floor, acting shy and backwards, making everyone uncomfortable that I had come down off the mountain.

I also knew how to speak wood-hick: "I got me a job at the Piggly Wiggly but my mamma didn't never get me one of those Social Security numbers, and they say I needs one to work."

And then there was the phrase that always put an end to every agent's curiosity about why I didn't already have one: "I's homeschooled … *by my daddy*." Nobody was crossing into that shit.

TCBY

I had only acquired three loans when my mother found an envelope of cash in the trunk of the Mustang.

She said, "Explain."

And I said, "I have a job at the yogurt store. I've had it for three, maybe four months now. Didn't I tell you?" *Stupid, stupid thing to say.* She didn't believe it, and it didn't account for the cash anyway, but I still had to go apply for work with TCBY to cover myself.

The frozen yogurt shop was in the neighboring city, Tullahoma, and the community there didn't yet know me. Outside my family's ceramic business, it was my first paying job and it was awful. I didn't know how anyone expected me to simply stand behind the counter and wait for a customer. And then once they came, it didn't get any more entertaining. The whole of the exchange rarely moved far beyond vanilla or chocolate. I was only two weeks in and my head was shrieking with boredom.

For no other reason than to break up the monotony, I faked a robbery.

I knew I could get away with it because people trusted me. The description most often applied to me was that of an angel. My history teacher broke mid lecture to stare at me and confess, "I can't stop myself from calling you angel face."

He wasn't the only one. I often heard of my angelic features. My expression was practiced innocence which inspired faith, so it was no surprise to me that in the first week of my employment with TCBY, I had been given keys to the store and the combination to the safe. As long as I held the angel mask firmly over my demonic smile, no one doubted my honesty.

I was supposed to be opening the store, but instead I picked up the phone and dialed 911. Barely keeping my voice together, I told the operator I had been threatened with a knife and had given away all the cash.

The money in the safe hadn't been deposited in a week, so the theft was substantial. Not that I needed it, I just couldn't abide the drudgery of serving frozen cones that day.

But after the commotion of squad cars and detectives, the tedium returned and I still had a job. And worse, I had played my distressed self so well that the manager of the store was constantly fawning over me in tears, and the police kept coming in to ensure I felt safe, treating me with such doting compassion that I felt sick with guilt for raising their emotions. When it all became too dramatic, and I had been hugged just one time too many, I threw down my heavenly mask and started laughing at the police chief.

There was no warning before the change. One week into the investigation, I was sitting in the chief's office with him and another detective going over mug shots, and then midsentence—*swoosh*—the white robes fell off.

I looked up to them slightly crazed, started laughing at their questions, and entirely ceased to take anything seriously. It was such a

171

drastic transformation, they looked genuinely concerned and asked if I had consumed any drugs, but I swore I hadn't.

I was still contending I had been robbed, but I was smirking through my every response, eyes locked on them in merriment, making certain they understood it was a game where I wanted to be chased.

They asked again if I had taken any drugs but I assured them, "No, this isn't drugs."

"Well, it's something." It had to be because I was clearly deranged.

Finally, they accused me of what I'd done, and while they could see it made me happy, I wouldn't admit it. I just smiled like a devil while insisting, "It was absolutely terrifying." Protesting, "I don't know why you won't believe me." And then wiping away nonexistent tears, "I was robbed at knife point."

I was being an infuriating little bitch, and the saner half of me was stepping back waving away any association with the lunatic.

The police chief warned he was getting multiple search warrants. He'd start with my car, and if he didn't find the money there, he wouldn't stop until my boyfriend's parents' house was overturned.

I had my mother's suspicions to contend with, so the money was already buried, and with thirty acres to my parents' property, I had no fear anyone would find it. All the forged and illicitly gained documents of identification were either concealed in the roof of the barn or at Mittwede's house, and Mittwede wasn't my boyfriend.

The police chief's threat to obtain warrants got a ridiculing laugh but nothing else.

He began to rage, informing me, "I will get you because I always get my suspect. Not once have I ever failed to get my suspect." He told me about the other clever little people that thought they could outfox him and how he had trapped them, arrested them, and sent them to jail.

He was bragging and I was taunting, "Why, I think you've frightened me."

He carried on to explain that I would confess, I would break, it may take him months, but he would dog my every move, pulling me out of class for questioning, asking for the details again and again until I slipped, made a mistake, and then I'd fall apart. He promised. "You will cry and I will be there when you do."

I looked him up and down with derision. "You are going to do all that *and* make me cry?" Just what kind of super-cop did he think he was? My disbelief turned to gleeful condescension, and I was choking on my amusement to ask, "Cry? Oh god, really? Cry? *You* think you can make *me* cry?" That was so particularly, demonically funny, I fell into laughing hysterics.

I hadn't exactly come out of Dallas unscarred. Sergiu had left his mark.

And of course the police chief was wrong, but he'd made his bold declaration before knowing about the list of investigators and the psychopath that had come before him.

The Shelbyville Police Department took the time to educate him, faxing him a newspaper article with which to confront me. I wondered who had scrawled "good luck!" in the corner.

After that, the police chief had a more modest view of his abilities. He had to settle with warning most of Tullahoma's businesses not to hire me if I applied, but I had no intention of getting another job. Mittwede did though. He'd been searching for new employment ever since the police chief told the management of Domino's Pizza that their driver, John Mittwede, was friends with a thieving criminal.

"You got me fired," Mittwede said. "And because they think you'll do it again, no one will hire me."

That was a truly unexpected consequence. I had walked away from the crime free and uncharged, but Mittwede was being punished. I grimaced, "Sorry."

But he wouldn't accept it. "You can't say you're sorry for something you won't admit doing."

"I can't?"

"No, you can't."

"Well, then, I can offer you money."

"I bet you can. And I bet is smells like a TCBY waffle cone."

"Some of it. But some of it smells like dirt."

"Dirt?" Mittwede looked aghast. His next question was an accusation, "Did you rob a grave?"

"Now there's an idea." Before he turned any paler, I assured him, "No, I wasn't digging into coffins. After all those threats of

174

search warrants, I decided it would be wise to take up a discreet hobby. I call it midnight gardening."

"Midnight gardening," he turned the phrase around a couple times and decided he liked it.

"Mmm," I agreed it was a nice expression. "All it takes is a shovel, a flashlight and a bag of valuables."

Mittwede didn't want to laugh and encourage me, but he suggested, "Why don't you go out tonight and see if you can dig up my rent."

PASSPORT SERVICES

The biggest prize in legitimate government-issued identification was the passport. Nothing else could top it. It was the undisputed confirmation of identity, and I wanted desperately to prove it could be fraudulently attained.

I was hovering over Mittwede this time, insisting the birth certificate had to be perfect. And by perfect I meant abused. It needed to look nineteen years old, the details plunked out with inconsistent strength on a manual typewriter, the ink saturated into the paper, and the paper needed to be discolored by age, and the edges softened with time.

We needed two pens. The mother and father could have shared one, but the doctor would have used something expensive that he kept in his shirt pocket.

It was the second time Amanda Palmer had a birth certificate created. The first time had been shortly before the yogurt incident. I had used Mittwede's original certificate to procure a license, but looking at the forgery again, I wondered if it was good enough for Passport Services. We could have started again from nothing, imagining a whole new name, but I didn't want to spend months aging another license. I knew it would look suspicious to apply for two IDs in the same week, so the license had to have a bit of age on it. Years would have been preferable, but I didn't want to wait that long, so instead, I was applying for the passport after only having the license for three months.

The birth certificate was from Alabama and the license from Tennessee. The address on the form was to a dilapidated farm house I passed everyday on the back roads to campus. The place was visible from the highway, so to appease the postman, I spent a day hanging curtains in the windows and placing two ferns on the porch. Then, the front door had to be propped back into place and both it and the mailbox painted.

Everything seemed perfectly sorted.

But the application never made it far enough to be delivered.

I learned there were some differences to acquiring a passport and a license.

At the Driver's License Service Center, there's the issue of time. People were waiting and you were expected to walk out of the center with a license on the same day. But the most desirable aspect of this arrangement was you got to stand in front of the agent and keep their attention diverted with how absolutely sweet and charming you were. Being the very essence of innocence, your birth certificate was obviously as genuine as you were.

Passport Services were far away and only saw a face on a photograph. Charm didn't play into it. And those bastards were also highly trained to spot fraud. They had lots of time to keep passing the forms along until someone called bullshit.

The letter in the newly painted mailbox was asking for more proof to support my application. But they weren't getting anything

177

else from me, and I wasn't sticking around for them to build a case. There was nothing to do but walk away and ignore it.

"The only concern," I told Mittwede, "is they have my picture."

"Only concern," he repeated. Pretty soon he had his arms wrapped around his guts and was rocking himself. He was certain, "We're going to be arrested."

"Nah."

"Oh, we are so fucked."

"It's not that bad."

"I don't want to go to jail."

"Calm down. If the worst happens, only I will be arrested."

"They'll know I helped."

"I don't break. They will never learn."

"They'll figure it out."

"How?"

"Who else do you hang out with?"

Well, there was that. I didn't seem to have any other friends.

A few days later, I arrived at his house to smell burning plastic and electronics. It was early afternoon and a plume of black smoke was rising from the field behind the garage. When I saw the printer and computer melting in a bonfire, I said, "Glad to see you're keeping it together. I don't imagine this will draw anyone's attention."

"I was losing it yesterday knowing every cop in five surrounding counties knows your face because you drive like a tornado, but this morning I go to pay for breakfast and there, right there at the Kroger check-out, staring me in the face is a national magazine with your picture on the cover. Counterfeit Countess, it said. In great big, bold type: Counterfeit! Countess! *Counterfeit*," he reiterated, "a word interchangeable with forgery and often associated with arrest."

Ah, yes. Patrice had called from Austin and warned me she had sold the story to *Woman's World* magazine.

"Last sentence?" Mittwede asked. "You know what it is?'

"No, I've not seen it."

"Tanya says, 'I'm going to grow up and be a con artist.'"

It had struck me as pretty funny when I said it, but Mittwede had better delivery. I think it was the hysteria.

He was saying, "I remember that story. That was like a year and a half ago. You didn't tell me you were *that* girl, the Dallas Countess. I already knew the story but I read it again, and I know all the cops have read it again, too. And now your picture is with Passport Services *and* at the check-out counter. You think federal agents don't buy groceries? You're fucking crazy. We're going to be arrested."

"You maybe need to take a Valium."

"I threw them all in the fire!"

~~~~~

Coming out sixteen months after my return home, Patrice had warned the article might be a little disruptive to my life, but I wasn't worried. It was *Woman's World*, not *Time* or *Newsweek*. Who read *Woman's World*?

Apparently everyone when you recognize the picture as a fellow student. I walked onto campus having the magazine thrust in my hand and asked for autographs.

"Are you serious?" Who asks for autographs?

About two hundred people do. But I was too mortified by the attention to respond.

After a week, I returned. The interest had died down to just the few women who would ask, "Why did you do it?"

And I would explain, "I was bored," but I knew this was an answer they couldn't understand.

I also had the attention of my male classmates. They would stare when they thought I was unaware, drifting off into a daze until the teacher called them all back with, "If only I were as interesting as Tanya." And then most of them needed to shift the car keys in their pants pockets.

That went on for weeks. In the library, an older student struck up a friendly chat that ended when he gave me a book by the Marquis de Sade and said, "I read the *Woman's World* article. You might like this. My number is in the front."

I sat slack-jawed at the library table wondering if the words really were arranged in the order I was seeing. *Give enough monkeys typewriters and they'll write Shakespeare*, they said. Well this monkey had banged out something evil. It was a struggle to read, but I got a few pages in, started skimming and flipping and then read the scene where the Marquis filled a couple of women's vaginas with boiling water.

My brain skidded out. I was rambling silently in my head, "He poured boiling water in them. He poured boiling water *into* them. The water was boiling. It specifically said boiling. I think that would kill someone. That would definitely kill someone. I'm pretty certain those women died. That's … that's … I don't know what that is."

But somebody thought I would like it.

His interest felt sinister, but I wrote it off thinking it was just another unusual attempt by the older men to grab my attention. One of them must have heard I liked to charge horses because he gave me a gift wrapped riding crop.

He was so confident when he presented it to me, and I loved getting gifts, even from people I seldom spoke with. I was all smiles until I got the paper off and then I was livid. My voice was outraged, "I have *never* hit my horse. *Never*. She goes fast because she wants to."

"You don't understand …"

"No, *you* don't understand: you don't hit animals. If the only way you have to communicate with them is through violence, then you're too stupid to be out of the trees."

It was a high stance to take when there were so few humans I could relate to. Mittwede had let his paranoia chase him to Atlanta and he wasn't coming back until, "I know that magazine is so long gone you can't even find a copy on the bottom of a bird cage."

CHANGING FOCUS

I had plenty of acquaintances and admirers, but Mittwede was my only friend, and I'd scared him off to Georgia. There were so few people I actually liked, and even fewer that were completely comfortable with me, so I knew if I got another, I would have to take better care of them. They would need to be protected from my antics.

And I already had someone's attention.

At first he unnerved me. His interest was fixed and intense, his eyes steady. And he didn't care if I caught him staring, he wouldn't look away. Six-foot-two and built like a Greek statue, he was hard to overlook. He was large, muscular, and perfectly formed, and this made him daunting, but there was something else unsettling about him, something too charming and powerful.

The only reason he wasn't outright frightening was because absolutely everyone on campus, and everyone in Tullahoma, seemed to know him, and they all genuinely adored him.

After four years away, he'd just returned home from the Marine Corps and people were excited to see him. Every time I saw him, another half dozen people would have spotted him and they'd race to him, calling, "Ed, oh my god, you're back."

Small crowds were constantly forming around him.

I was keeping my distance but I was watching, and he'd talk to his innumerable friends but stare at me. The same scene played out repeatedly in the library, the cafeteria, and the theater, and then finally off campus at a pizza parlor.

He was clear of the table, sitting in the center of the restaurant, holding court. The chairs around him were never empty but his audience kept changing. It was appealing because he wasn't arrogant in the least. He was laughing and sincere, and it was plainly evident he was loved and people wanted to be near him, but he still made me nervous.

The place was crowded. Several groups were standing, and people were packed so tight together they were forced to shift to allow others to pass through. If you entered the scrum, you were completely at the mercy of where they directed you, and they funneled me to Ed.

Stepping past him, I felt his hands on my hips and then I was in his lap.

The move had been effortless. After an exchange of smiles, we said nothing. I just relaxed against his chest and he wrapped an arm around my waist, then we sat for several minutes without speaking. It felt perfectly natural, even right, to be there.

Finally, he said, "We should go for a ride. I have a second helmet on my bike."

I loved to charge, and Ed rode like he was late for the battle. The highway was full of bends yet the speedometer was buried, and the engine was still able to kick up speed in the straights. The wind was battering him harder than me, and I had to keep my face hidden behind his back. When we finally turned onto the back roads, I thought he would slow to a cruise, but he would only brake to a hundred to take the curves. We were leaning so low that if I had dared let go of him, I could have run my farthest hand over the asphalt.

There was no doubt in my mind we were going to die, and it was going to be spectacularly gory. I was certain the fire department would have to be called to wash away the trail of blood, and our skin would probably be splayed across the barbed wire fences that lined the road. I was just hoping that when the flesh was ripped off my bones, I would already be gone.

I had just turned seventeen and thought it was a pity I would perish so young, and without having proved a passport could be attained with a forged birth certificate too.

As Ed swerved around one curve, I remembered I had never gone back to Nashville to finish a half completed bank loan, and on another curve, I wished I had told Mittwede where all the money was buried.

The hour-long ride gave me a chance to reflect on my activities and my first year of college. I'd not taken it very seriously. I'd not proved to anyone that I was smart, or made grades that supported the designation of genius. I'd skipped class, failed history, and convinced Mittwede to do an instructional video for communications class titled *How to Make Bathtub Barbiturates*.

I wasn't a good student and I wasn't a good friend. I'd lost Mittwede his job and his future prospects, then, before he could be suspended from college for violating the code of ethics, I'd forced him to flee to Atlanta for fear of being charged with felony forgery.

If at any time in the past year I'd been particularly clever, it had only been with bank managers, Social Security agents, and licensing officials, and that wasn't the sort of thing my family would inscribe on my headstone.

It would probably just read: *Here lies Tanya. She could be charming.*

I wouldn't need a very big space because I doubted they'd be able to scrape up much of what remained, and a lot of me would probably be buried with Ed.

We were going to go out as one indistinguishable smear of blood, gore and bike parts on an old country road, killed by a combination of speed and testosterone, loose gravel, and maybe even a wandering farm animal.

By the time the ride was over, I'd envisioned fifty types of death, confronted my destructive nature, regretted the harm done to Mittwede as well as my wasted potential, then accepted my fate along with my mortality, and was left too exhausted to feel any further fear.

I stepped off Ed's bike at the pizza parlor and started stumbling around the parking lot, struggling to get the helmet off but too weak from repeated adrenaline attacks to manage it. I was pretty certain I had lost a couple of my senses on the ride. Sight and sound seemed to be limited to the helmet.

The sense of touch returned when Ed tore back the Velcro strap under my chin and I was finally able to free myself from the headpiece.

Ed was laughing.

I had just enough composure left to be defensive. "I've never ridden on a bike before."

He said, "I know. I had to compensate on the curves because you were fighting it."

"It was terrifying."

"But you liked it." He was smiling because he knew it was true.

It took a moment for me to realize, "It was…" I couldn't admit erotic, so said instead, "…amazing."

"Do you want to do it again?"

"Oh my god, yes. But faster."

~~~~~~

I was so completely possessed with Ed, I forgot all about the birth certificates and Social Security numbers. The allure of banks and fraudulent loans lost its dominant place in my mind. And it was no longer so important to procure that last elusive piece of genuine federally recognized identification when Ed could move me so much further than Passport Services.

I could barely remember a thing I had been doing before meeting him, and everything I had done shortly after turning sixteen was so distant as to be another lifetime; so I was particularly taken aback to get the letter from the United States Navy telling me the date I needed to show up to ship-out for basic training.

That had been a crazy Saturday. I couldn't quite recall what had possessed me to run off and join the Navy, but I'd taken the tests, passed the exams, and sworn the oath before noon.

The recruiting agent had been incredibly helpful, telling me I didn't need parental permission if I enrolled in the Delayed Entry Program. Being sixteen, I could spend the next year finishing high school, or in my case, accumulating college credits, and I wouldn't have to worry about basic training until six months before I turned eighteen.

I called the same recruiting agent and told him a lot had happened in the last eighteen months, and, "Regarding this whole Navy business, I've changed my mind."

He laughed before realizing it wasn't a joke. "You can't change your mind. You already signed and swore an oath. You are a United States soldier. Let me make this clear: You will be arrested by the military police and thrown in the brig if you fail to show up."

Oh.

Ed was staring at me aghast. "You did what?"

"I was bored one weekend and joined the Navy."

"How could you forget?"

"Well, I didn't so much forget as not think about it again."

"They *will* arrest you."

"I guess I won't be bored that weekend."

"Tanya?"

"Yes?"

"Do you understand this is serious?"

"I suspected it was."

Then the certified letter arrived telling me to turn myself in. The recruiting agent had been calling me Mario Andretti because of the number of speeding tickets I had acquired, and he warned the next time I was pulled over, I'd be taken into custody.

That could happen at any moment. The cops had me on the side of the road at least once a month. I'd charm my way out of most of the tickets and laugh my way into the rest. I was just one point away from losing my license but even so, I couldn't drive the speed limit. Ed knew this. He said, "They won't make you serve if you get married."

It was a strange way to propose, but I loved that it wasn't sentimental or emotional.

Four months before my eighteenth birthday, two months after I should have shipped off to the Navy, Ed and I had a big church wedding.

It made not the slightest bit of difference to the Navy, but by the time they found us again in Memphis, they had given up. They sent a letter dismissing me of all obligations, but also warned I was not eligible to enter any of the other services. I was glad to hear it, too, because I still had a problem with boredom and there was no telling what I might get up to.

THE CASTLE

From the very beginning, Ed was warned against me.

"She's trouble," was the general opinion, as was, "You're going to regret it."

"She's a bit of a rogue," was the affectionate version of "She's an unrepentant criminal." And, "There's something wrong with her," was the polite way of saying, "She's fucking crazy."

Most people that loved Ed feared I would do something that would either result in his arrest or his death.

But Ed's psychology professor had a more specific concern. "She will do it again," he said. "Once a runaway, always a runaway." It was a certainty. "Maybe not tomorrow or even this year, but she'll encounter some stress she doesn't want to face and then," *snap*, "she'll be gone. Why? Because she's a runaway and that's what runaways do."

The same professor had me as a student the previous year so he felt confident saying, "She's not stable. Oh, she's intelligent, but once you cross over 150 IQ, there is guaranteed psychosis. And what you've got in Tanya is over 170 with a history of psychotic behavior." He was shaking his head, "I wouldn't do it."

Ed had also tested well over the safety threshold, but the madness wasn't the same.

We had been married for six years when Ed demanded, "Do you know the difference between neurotics and psychotics?" He answered before I could speak, "Neurotics build castles in the sky; psychotics move into them."

And there was no denying I'd made an unholy mess of the place either, but he'd invited me in and then locked all the doors. The invitation alone was foolish, but it became downright stupid when he took the keys and left.

Nearly everyone he knew tried to warn him, "She is up to something. She's not the type you can leave alone and expect to behave."

I even tried to threaten him, "You keep ignoring me and we're both going to regret it."

But he didn't believe any of it. He was a counselor at a wilderness program for juvenile delinquents and he loved his work. It was where he most wanted to be. He would spend weeks in the woods, and then come home for two days to recuperate. He spent most of the two days sleeping and the rest of it meeting with other counselors to discuss the week.

He needed to spend the moments he was awake processing the emotional events of his job, but he couldn't talk with me because I always sided with the kids. I was an anarchist and his authoritarian rule over them was tyranny. Why they didn't all run away was a mystery to me.

"Because they would be caught," Ed said.

"No they wouldn't," I scowled. "They're not idiots."

He became patronizing. "It's not easy to run away. If you'd been placed out there, you wouldn't have been able to run away either. You'd have been caught if you tried."

The insult was extreme and I was livid. "I'll remind you, I *did* run away and no one caught me. And you might want to think about who I was playing with before you make another claim that you could do better."

Every now and again, Ed needed to be knocked back.

He knew from the start I was a con artist. He knew I was a criminal. He knew shortly after we met that I had already assumed more names than I could remember, and he knew when he made me promise to never do it again that I couldn't.

When he finally learned what I had been up to, he blamed me for psychotically destroying his neurotic fantasies.

"You built the castle," I accused. "I am not responsible for its structural integrity."

~~~~~~~

Ed learned that even the most stable structure can't survive a sustained attack against the foundation. I'd been lighting fires in the cellar against the powder kegs for years, and when the damage tore down the walls, I asked to move out. I wanted a divorce. But I wanted to make the parting painless. I needed him to want me out, so every time he suggested a repair, I would recall a small fire I had set.

"Did I tell you about the time I rented a house in Fayetteville and ran about sixty thousand in credit under a stranger's name?"

He looked away, murmuring, "No."

"It was last year, right around my twenty-third birthday. I was intending to send her the diamond bracelet to make amends, but then I thought it would just freak her out."

"That bracelet is real?"

"Yeah," it almost sounded like an apology. "I told you it was silver and cubic zirconia, but it's actually platinum and diamond."

We were going on the third week since I had first tried to get him to evict me, and he knew I would keep sharing details until he hung his head in defeat and admitted, "Stop. It's over. I see that."

But then the next day, he recovered and offered again, "We can fix it."

I felt forced to counter with, "Do you know about the week I took a job in Columbia just to clear out the company safe? I can't even remember what name I used, there's been so many."

It was taking less and less to drop his head.

"It amazes even me that I can continue to call up a new incident every time you falter. I wonder how many more times we can do this?"

"I wonder, too." But he continued to try. "I forgive all you've done."

"You recall the time the sheriff came to arrest you for bank fraud? Sorry about that. My mistake. But you have to give me credit, I did fix it before he could get the cuffs on you."

"Dear God, Tanya, what did I do to deserve such dishonesty?"

"Hard to say, but whatever it was, it must have been pretty bad."

"We'll start over."

192

"Did you know the car in the backyard is stolen?"

"I still love you."

"The lock picks you found were actually mine. Do you want to know how I used them?"

"No. I'm done. You've made your point. It's over."

And still, I could have gone on for weeks. I could have told him things that would have burned the roof, razed the walls, and blasted the rubble into dust.

~~~~~~

It had started with a storm. It so often did. The systems moving in would rip through my skull, blinding me with migraines, enraging me with pain that would last for days and sometimes weeks while I waited for the rains to come. My head could predict the weather like a satellite image. I knew the severity of what was coming by whether it made me retch, and I didn't always mind because the worst headaches disappeared almost instantly with the lightning. The dramatic release would ensure a rush of euphoria that was exhilarating and I'd want to do something.

But I had promised I wouldn't. So for a long time, I didn't.

Then Ed went into the woods and I was alone. And I was bored. And there was only one thing I wanted to do. It was the only passion I had besides Ed.

It was 3:00 a.m. and I was in a manic state of desire. The power had just gone out when lightning hit a transformer. Abruptly my head was clear and a lot of plans were flooding my thoughts, but with them came quite a few questions.

Legitimate identification and what you could do with it still possessed me, and of late, the mailbox was filled with pre-approved applications for credit.

I studied the form in candlelight. It seemed a weak system, one easily foiled by nothing more than a date of birth and Social Security number, and both were easy to come by. But I wasn't certain about the fallout, and I didn't want to ruin a stranger's life.

I decided to test out the scheme on myself.

The first question was, "How much credit can be accumulated in a month?" It was 1993 and everyone was eager to give me plastic, so the answer was a little over fifty thousand and I hadn't been trying.

Then I wondered, "How do the creditors know it was me that applied for it?"

The answer was clear, they didn't know, and based on how easy it was, they really didn't care.

So in three days, I ran every line of credit to its max and when the bills came, I called the banks and said, "I didn't apply for this and I didn't use it."

"The card was sent to your address," was the sole argument in security.

"No one has been home for months," was my defense. "It was identity fraud."

Now the biggest question: What were the consequences?

I wouldn't steal anyone's identity if the repercussions were anything worse than inconvenience. Ed had diagnosed me wrong: I was a sociopath but I was *not* a psychopath.

I understood right from wrong, I just didn't care. I was even capable of guilt, though no one believed it. No one had seen me display it. But I always questioned, "Why would I do something that is going to make me feel guilty?" I wouldn't. Not intentionally. It made no sense.

Consequently, I'd only financially hit banks and businesses covered by insurance. I didn't care if they were rich or poor, I didn't score money from individuals.

So I needed to confirm with the recent credit scam that the name on the card would not be held accountable. And it wasn't. All the banks required to clear the balance was a police report. That was nothing.

I sat in the police chief's office again wondering if I was finally going to pay for my laughing insolence, but the chief had retired and the detectives had forgotten all about me and TCBY. They were incredibly sympathetic, the report was filed, and then it was like it had never happened.

I wasn't certain how I felt about it.

The success of my cons was not so much determined by money, but by the swath of destruction I left behind. It was measured by what I had managed to escape or survive.

And this had been too simple. Nothing had gone wrong. There hadn't been a single moment when I felt like the deception was slipping away from me or was getting out of control. It didn't feel satisfying.

I wanted chaos. I wanted to be chased. I wanted to be questioned, suspected, respected, and loathed. I wanted to fight for my life and liberty. More than anything, I wanted the pleasure of fear. It had been entirely too many years since I had known it.

I would eventually steal someone's identity to run a line of credit, but only to prove it was too easy. I did it to add to the mayhem of everything else I was doing, all in an attempt to tip my life over into pandemonium, looking for the thrill of being overwhelmed and challenged, hoping someone would pursue so I could run.

WEEPING WILLOW

There had been a fair number of storms during the two years Ed was at the wilderness program. I had spent a quarter of it with screaming migraines tearing out my eyes, and the other three-quarters resuming my experiments with creating legitimate identification.

Things had changed. Social Security had now become our de facto identification number. All private services and utilities could be denied if you didn't surrender it upon request. I was furious it had happened and had spent years fighting it. I always declined to give mine or would give obviously false numbers, like a string of nine fives in a row. I'd explain the Unites States was not a police state and the law was clear that our Social Security number was strictly between us and Social Security. I warned that if we continued to submit to the request, it would be tattooed on our wrists. I'd encourage others to fight with me, to refuse or sabotage, or even just whine a bit, but they all had the same line: "If you're not doing anything wrong, you have nothing to hide."

I hated them.

They would say, "You're like my grandfather, getting mad when the state started requiring pictures on driver's licenses. He said it wouldn't amount to nothing but an incursion on our rights. But he was wrong; it prevents anyone else from using it. The pictures keep us safe."

And I'd clinch my teeth so not to speak.

"Same with the Social Security number. It will make it near impossible for people to defraud the banks, hospitals, and insurance companies. And that's good, because we all pay the price when they're taken advantage of."

I wanted to rip their stupid patronizing heads off.

"But you're young," they'd say. "One day you'll understand the world isn't safe. People take advantage. You're just too angel-faced sweet to know any better."

It was all I could do not to tear apart their lives just to prove the angels weren't on their side.

But it was my own fault. I'd spent years perfecting the image of innocence. I only got speeding tickets when I couldn't be bothered to cry, and I could make a Social Security agent weep genuine tears that I had been raised by antiestablishment hippies in a bus.

It explained the name: Willow.

But I hadn't made this one up. I had a genuine birth certificate. She'd been buried with her parents in a cemetery with five headstones. The place sat in a farmer's field and was surrounded by a low iron fence that had fallen into pieces decades before. The oldest graves were from the turn of the century and sat square center of the plot, but then this family of three with a different last name had knocked down one side of the railings to be fitted in. They shared a single, wide marker with the dates of death just one day apart and the year was seventy-four. The child, like me, would have been four.

Her death, chiseled between mother and father, kept bringing me back. I was glad her parents were dead. I had two deceased brothers and knew most intimately what it did to a family to lose a child. But here it seemed they had been wiped out together and I hoped the mother that had lived an extra day never knew.

Every now and again, I would show the place to someone, and we would wonder what had happened to them. I was certain it had been a road accident and finally went to the newspaper to search the dates, but the family wasn't even in the death notices. I asked the property owner, but they'd only bought the farm in the last decade and didn't know. The oldest neighbors said the former owner had let the fields lay fallow, but I wouldn't find her as she'd passed many years before. They thought the graves had something to do with a family reunion.

Blessed hell, that turned it dark.

I was now fully committed to learning the story and was prepared for anything from shotguns to food poisoning. I suspected it had happened in a state park, because that's where family reunions take place, so I started searching the libraries on the way to each wide open pavilion with a bar-b-que, scanning the old newspaper microfilms for their names.

As first suspected, it was a car accident. The father's death certificate was in the county courthouse, but the mother and child's were not. I understood what I was seeing. They had been transported to a larger city with a better hospital and I knew where to go. They were an hour away, but the couple didn't share the same last name as the tombstone suggested. Each came from a different city outside the state.

Something about them seemed too tragic to ignore, but my interest in them was purely macabre. At least until I saw the child's death certificate. It didn't list her place of birth. It was unknown.

It meant her birth certificate was clean.

And I had to have it. She had to live again. I wouldn't do anything bad with her, no check kiting or credit card fraud, or anything to sully her name. I'd likely just set her aside, bury her again in my box of stolen names and illicit valuables. I had loved her for ages and now I'd take care of her.

But first I had to find her.

I had a good idea of where to go for that too.

Her birth notice was in her mother's home paper and her birth certificate was in county records. I arrived at the court house looking like a starry-eyed Deadhead, smelling of patchouli, bells jangling on my ankles, smiling peace and wonder at the Southern conservative clerks. Against my chest was a clearly visible gold cross.

I had to explain why I had no identification to claim my birth certificate, but the face of an angel never lies and it was really very simple. I'd lived my whole life in a psychedelic bus following the Grateful Dead from one city to the next. My parents were New Age mystics sitting in lotus and meditating on Shiva; but at a Kentucky concert, a Baptist preacher came to denounce our wicked ways and I went down on my knees to accept the Lord.

"Bless your heart," the woman behind the counter whispered and then, "Jesus be praised, you found your way."

The birth certificate was mine and she was confiding, "I can always tell a good soul."

~~~~~~

Willow was in a midnight garden under the hickories. I'd buried her in the backyard in the dark hours of morning, and I dug her up six months later at noon. It looked like dusk though. Overhead two systems were colliding and the pain in my head predicted tornadoes. The wind was on the verge of drawing blood, pelting me with nuts and broken twigs, kicking up scattered leaves and grass, and whipping my hair across my face until it stung. My eyes were red and full of tears, and I was nearly blind, but I wasn't crying.

I was done with crying. I was battling the wind now and everything it threw at me. It was fierce and cutting, but I didn't care. It wasn't anything worse than what was screeching through my skull, and it was definitely preferable to Ed's indifference.

I'd been begging him for more than a year to listen to me, to understand we would soon be over if he didn't pay attention to me. I couldn't be ignored. I wouldn't stay home alone any longer. But he said our relationship was too strong for me to do anything. We were too deeply connected for it to end.

"And right now," he said, "the juvenile delinquents at the wilderness program need stability. As their counselor, I have to be there for them."

And I had to get away. The rains were coming and with them would come the release and the ecstasy, and I'd use the high not to think about what I was doing. I wasn't exactly running away, I was just leaving without mentioning it. And I wasn't too certain when I'd be back either. I had a shoulder bag of books and a carry-on, but that meant very little about the length of time I intended to roam. I traveled light. I'd taken only a fur coat, cash, and lipstick to Dallas, so in relative terms, I was packed for a lunar expedition.

I was back at the Nashville airport buying a ticket at the counter, unsettling the airline agent with my insistence, "I really don't care what city. I just want the next flight into Mexico," which was probably not the smartest thing to walk into an airport and say.

She looked suspicious.

I answered before she could ask, "No, I have not just robbed a bank." Though I did have someone else's name on my credit cards, and Willow's driver's license in my wallet.

She offered, "Cancun?"

And I threw my hands up, "Sure."

"Returning when?"

"I don't need a return."

"No return?" She had a good look at me and decided I was not escaping the law but something else. She became concerned, "Are you sure? A return ticket is invaluable."

I was less convinced, "I don't think I'll use it."

Fingers frozen over the keyboard, she was chewing her lips. Then without further warning, she reached across the counter for my hand, asking, "Are you alright?"

That was the last question I needed to be asked. I stepped back before she made me cry. I would have agreed to anything. "A return is great."

She withdrew. "It will make going through immigration easier."

"Lovely. I'll take it."

"When?"

"Oh ... Um ... Well ... Hmm ..."

"Let's just make the return for a week and you can change it if you need. Okay?"

"Okay."

MEXICO

It was my second day in Cancun and I was sitting alone at an outdoor café in the city's tourist district, but I was never alone for long. I had no problem traveling by myself because people always reached out to draw me in. This time it was a table of three Mexican men. They were in their late twenties or early thirties, immaculately dressed, and laden with gold.

We chatted across the café until one extended the invitation, "Come join us." Then when I took a seat, he introduced the table, "I am Miguel. This is Hector and Ramiro."

"And I'm Willow."

Ten minutes later, I was explaining, "I hate to dash anyone's hopes, but I prefer women."

They reacted by pulling back in astonishment. Hector asked, "Lesbian?"

And I smiled, "Yes." I could have told them I was married, but I'd found marriage did little to dissuade men's interest. Nothing quite shifted the dynamics like saying women were preferable. I always ceased to be a potential conquest and became instead a strange member of the team. *We're all after pussy here.*

While they spoke amongst themselves in Spanish, I stared at the traffic passing on Boulevard Kukulcan. There was a steady stream of taxis, buses, and rentals on the road, and the sidewalks were busy with young American tourists.

I had no idea what the three men were saying, except they were rearranging their plans with regard to me. After much amusement, Ramiro left the table smiling, and then his friends and I continued to converse over drinks.

We were talking about the Mayan ruins that were a couple of hours outside Cancun when Ramiro returned. On each arm he had nearly identical blonds that stood a foot taller than him. I'd never seen anything like them. Not in the flesh. Everything about them was exaggerated. Each strand of hair was the same unnatural color, teased to a height that made them four inches taller, and their lips were abnormally large, freakishly plump and painted in high gloss pink to match their miniskirts and six-inch heels. As they moved closer, I felt the need to push back to give their breasts room at the table. I studied their faces and thought they had to be Americans, but I couldn't tell if they were pretty because they seemed like another species.

And they had a shared expression that was as practiced vacant as mine was innocent.

"Bunny and Candy," Ramiro gave them names.

He pulled up chairs and settled them on either side of himself, which put the rabbit next me. He leaned around the great swell bursting from the stressed buttons of Bunny's chest, motioning me forward to whisper, "I brought this one for you."

"Did you say bought or brought?"

"¿Cómo?"

"Never mind." I pulled back to look at her and she laid her vacuous eyes on me to smile.

"Thank you, Ramiro, how very thoughtful."

Then two quick hops and she had scooted her chair closer to mine, dragging Ramiro and the clone with her.

And I swallowed a disconcerted laugh.

The restaurant was filling as the sun began to set and I was searching its perimeter for a gracious excuse to leave. I'd played the homosexual card countless times before, but no one had ever thrown down two plastic chips to see my hand.

Sitting at the same table with them, watching their lips wrap around fat straws to suck at something pink, I no longer felt decidedly feminine. We were now a gathering of three men, two female caricatures, and an aberration.

I was a freakish anomaly until Katia arrived to balance it out. I was looking at the exit with longing as she entered, and she was taking in the whole scene at our table with disapproval. Her black hair was pulled into a ponytail which left her clean face exposed so that her expression was clear. Condemnation had narrowed her eyes, but there was no sign of surprise. She'd seen it before.

Miguel had ordered six shots and Katia stopped the waiter to add one more. She pulled a chair from an adjoining table and then kicked at Hector's feet until he made room for her to sit on my right.

She asked, "Ramiro, are you scaring the turista?"

"No, she likes. ¿Sí? You like?"

Smiling at no one in particular, I raised my rum and coke to murmur through the ice, "Mmm hmm mmm."

"Turista, look at me."

"Hmm?"

"You like Bunny?"

"Mmm hmm mmm." Then dropping the glass from my lips, "I don't think this is Bacardi."

I didn't mean for her to explode, but she sent Spanish like shrapnel across the restaurant to the bar, screaming something-something-something that sounded like she was going to eviscerate the bartender, and then something-something-Bacardi. The men at the table were sinking into their seats, covering their laughing embarrassment with gold-covered fingers, and the bartender was smiling guiltily while making two more rum and cokes from a newly opened bottle of Bacardi.

She was a mad general in the green zone, casually strolling in to call down artillery. The whole place was shell-shocked. Taking my half-finished drink, she downed it, exchanged it with the new drinks brought by the waiter, and while helping to disperse the tequila shots, she said to Bunny, "This is all you get."

And Bunny giggled, then whispered in Ramiro's ear.

I couldn't shoot tequila, or any other straight spirit. If I even dared to try, I would gag, vomit, and die of mortification. But I'd been handling this social quandary for some time, so when everyone else threw back, I tossed mine straight over my shoulder to splash on the sidewalk.

I'd been caught before. I'd endured outrage for slinging Jack Daniels into a crowd, shock for flinging Absolut across the carpet, and there'd been chaos with the flaming 151, but nothing quite compared to Katia. She had led this shot, so she was putting her empty glass down before the rest of us were finished. She caught my hand while it was still at my shoulder and held it there as evidence of wrongdoing, complete confusion scowling across her face. Then contrary to her expression, she grabbed the back of my head to force the absolute strangest kiss on me. Full, open mouth, passionate, I-want-to-fuck-you kiss.

We'd only just met. She hadn't even heard my name. I wanted to treat her like a man and be outraged, but the act was exquisite. Shocking, presumptive, and quite possibly wrong without consent, but it was definitely unique, and I can't help but respond to something pleasantly different.

I moaned an amazed, "Oh God," in her mouth, and then felt her lips smile. Without releasing the hold she had on my hair, she slid to my ear to whisper, "These guys are very rich," and Bunny started yanking at the arm of my chair, but Katia was still sharing, breathing into my neck, "We could have a great time at their villa." Now Bunny was pulling at my arm, trying to bring my attention around, and the men were laughing, speaking in Spanish while Katia looked around to shout, "Bunny, no," and then her breath was back against my neck, making me shiver, promising, "You will see things you have never seen."

I most desperately wanted to see things I had never seen, but I thought she should know, so I whispered back, "I'm not actually a lesbian."

"No importa, turista. If you like, I will make you one."

~~~~~

~~~~~

So far it was nothing I hadn't seen before or couldn't have imagined. We were at a stucco house wedged crooked and tight between more stucco houses off Boulevard Kukulcan. Across the street, the ocean filled a vast lagoon with still water, and boats were tied to a dock. The party had grown to include three giggling senior graduates from someplace wholesome like Nebraska. They were swimming drunk in their underwear, periodically looking around the backyard pool to ask, "Where are Bobby and Jake?"

Miguel repeatedly assured them, "They will be here soon," but after an hour, he no longer bothered to look at Hector with mischievous shame, and both had stopped silently shrugging, "Bobby and Jake?"

They didn't look particularly interested in the girls. It seemed more a matter of habit, like a night-cap, except the necessary conclusion to each evening was a few American teenagers.

Their attention was on the glass top table and the tray of cocaine. And my focus was with them. I had wanted to try it ever since reading *Diary of a Drug Fiend*, but the psychonauts Ed and I mixed with were users of marijuana and psychedelics. I'd done a fair amount of both, eating through several sheets of acid, choking down pounds of mushrooms, and swallowing more ecstasy than was decent, but no one we knew had a connection to cocaine.

I understood what it should do—Aleister Crowley's descriptions sounded quite merry—but I'd lift my head from Miguel's powder and feel nothing. I snorted line after line and only managed to numb my throat. My head remained utterly straight.

It was a problem I had with most new drugs. My brain had to learn how to get high. It had taken two years and several pounds of pot before I finally got stoned. In the meantime, I'd bong hit everyone to the floor and then drive them all home. And I could still tip a bottle of codeine with no effect. Hydrocodone was an aspirin and Xanax was a Tic-Tac.

But telling people this always seemed to cause offense, as though I were insulting the quality of their drugs. Not wanting to appear rude or ungrateful to my hosts, I didn't mention it. I just did every line Miguel put before me. And then everyone else would do a line. If I had recognized it was a contest to see who would quit first, I might have warned them, but it wasn't obvious until it was down to just two of us.

And we'd left the others in a terrible state. Hector was on the edge of his chair, rocking off the tips of his toes. He was making a high keening noise and I worried he was about to start screaming. I thought he might be freaking out over Katia. She'd been non-stop jabbering at him in manic Spanish, talking too fast to do any of the last four lines. And Candy was a panting wreck I couldn't look at. She'd had a quick burst of frantic self-destruction, ripping apart her hair and smearing lipstick across her face, and now her eyes were streaming mascara down her cheeks, but she wasn't crying. Bunny had dashed to the bathroom half an hour earlier, and I had no idea what condition she was in, but I was watching Ramiro run fully clothed into the pool while Miguel cut out more lines.

210

Miguel had no chance in this competition either. He was breathing heavy with the jitters and I was still hoping to feel something.

I drew up the offered line and Miguel finally gave up.

He said through clinched teeth, "You are fucking steady."

Hector's screech had settled into a quivering moan. He was still rocking but he paused to look at me and cross himself, incanting, "Ave María Purísima."

Ramiro was shivering in the pool, chattering out, "You win, guapa."

I asked, "Do I get to pick the prize?"

Hector dropped his head between his knees and turned hysterical, but I couldn't tell if it was laughter or a return high-pitched madness.

Miguel stopped rolling his jaw to ask, "What is the prize you want?"

"Show me something I've never seen before. Shock me. Surprise me. Blow my wee little mind. I don't care what you do, but let's not be boring."

~~~~~~

It probably would have been wiser to insult the cocaine. I'd thrown down the don't-bore-me gauntlet in a dangerous crowd. But after the cocaine episode, they were also a little afraid of me. It had taken them the rest of the night to get themselves straight, and while they did, the little Nebraskans were put into a cab.

I'd gone with Katia in Miguel's Mercedes to retrieve my suitcase and a shoulder bag of books from one of the big hotels on the beach. I didn't checkout, but I didn't think I was coming back either.

For a year, I had been asking myself, "What am I doing?" Questioning with each new identification made, "Do I want to do this?" But I'd rent a house and apply for credit regardless, wondering, "Does this make me happy?" Then for months, I'd collect cards, only stopping when the banks began to decline. In a day, I'd blow their limits, blasting through tens of thousands, doubting, "Is this even fun?"

I didn't know. I was pretty certain it used to be, back when I was sixteen and seventeen, in the time before Ed, before I had been exposed to the principles of psychology and mental awareness. Ed didn't believe the excuse that I was bored was the legitimate reason for my actions, but then he didn't believe the goal of life was to be entertained, and I did.

The objective was to be happy and amused, and whether that was achieved by self-awareness or breaking the law made no difference to me. Having done a bit of both, I was conscious that neither was thrilling me at the moment. And I was avoiding the one because I didn't want to observe my thoughts, or think about what I was doing in the rental houses, or to Ed, our marriage, or my mind.

I didn't want to dwell on what I was doing in Mexico either, but I knew I would see it through. Once I tipped over the edge of any action, the instant I gave a little and said, "Yes, sure, why not, let's do this," momentum carried it along.

Waking to a house full of strangers, I was already avoiding the question, "What am I doing with these people?" Trying not to look at Hector on the couch cleaning a gun. Ignoring the sounds of Bunny and Candy upstairs with Ramiro. None too crazy about Katia or screwdrivers for breakfast. And then there was Miguel, sitting next to Hector, facing Katia and I on the opposite couch, wanting to know, "What you said last night, is this something you still desire?"

It was all momentum, "Of course."

"¿Sí?"

"Sí."

He spoke to Katia and she silently left, going outside to sit beside the pool. Hector could not have gotten another speck off that gun but he continued brushing out the barrel, oiling the hammer and trigger, rubbing the muzzle with no intent of looking up. Miguel spoke to him and Hector nodded yes, then Miguel said to me, "I have a friend in Atlanta. I have for him something. You want to take this to him?"

They were asking me to smuggle drugs. How very unimaginative and yet classic. I said, "Of course," but knew I wouldn't.

"It is nothing bad."

"What a pity."

"¿Cómo?

"It would have been more fun if it were bad."

Miguel turned that around in his head for several seconds before offering, "Maybe you will return and I will have for you something bad."

213

"That would be lovely. Will you show me what it is that's going to Atlanta?"

Motioning to Hector, "We go. You stay. We will return with it."

There was no way they were not bringing back drugs. I was imagining a cliché Mary statue filled with cocaine and wondered what hilarious location would present itself for me to dump the thing before boarding the plane home. I was glad the agent had given me the return. I was only three days away and I wasn't sure I wanted to be in Cancun any longer. I wasn't sure where I wanted to be, but I'd take Mary as far as I dared.

I thought leaving her at the airport lounge amongst the bottles of cordials might be funny, but I didn't remember seeing a bar on my arrival. No worry though, I'd give her to the taxi driver, but then again, Miguel would probably want to drive me to the airport, maybe even see me off. I'd be forced to wipe her for fingerprints and leave her hidden in the plane before hitting US Customs. And I suppose hope his friend stayed in Atlanta and didn't meet me at the Nashville airport. But now that would be exciting. That would definitely be fun. He'd chase and I'd run and it would be satisfying.

GETTING TO KNOW YOU

It would be dark before Hector and Miguel returned. While they were gone, Bunny and Candy were sunning in lounge chairs, and Katia had me against the pool wall, telling me of her prowess in bed. "I can make you forget your name."

I'd forgotten my name once in a con. It was the single most panic-inducing moment of my life and I didn't want to experience it again. But Katia was reminding me, whispering, "Willow, you should trust me."

"I don't know that trust has anything to do with it." I knew Ed wouldn't care if I slept with a woman; we'd both done it before, but, "I just didn't get much out of it."

Katia lifted her mouth from my neck to ask, "Was she a lesbian or a girl playing?"

I had to concede, "In all cases it was an experiment between heterosexuals."

"Not a lesbian?"

"No."

"You understand the problem? Yes?"

I was beginning to. Her hands were on me with strength and urgency, not skimming my body softly like I had known, or like I was returning. She passionately wanted something and was trying to pull it into herself. Kissing to consume, holding to possess. And I had been neglected for so long, I was on the cusp of returning it.

I had said it so many times before, "If there were a pill that could make me a lesbian, I'd take two to make sure it stuck." I was sexually attracted to men, but sharing space with them was difficult. The desire to unite seemed like a sadistic joke on both sexes. A psychologist from the wilderness program summed it up as, "All men are pigs and all women think weird." It was crude and not exact, but it was essentially the essence of the problem.

I wondered if Katia was the pill. If I accepted her like a cure, even twice, would I be free of men? Or, at the very least, free of Ed?

I warned Katia, "I'm just a tourist, you understand."

"Yes, turista."

"I'm just sightseeing."

She laughed, kissed me harder and said, "Sí, turista. I am the tour guide."

~~~~~~

It had just turned dark and there was noise in the house. I listened to it move up the stairs and become quiet again. Leaving the room Katia was sleeping in for mine, I was glad to have been taught the difference between two girls playing and a genuine I-want-a-woman lesbian, but it hadn't cured me.

Light from my room was illuminating the hall, but I thought little of it until I stood in the open door. My carry-on had been dumped in the center of the bed and Ramiro was at the mirror with my bag of cosmetics, a shade of red coloring his top lip and brown

216

darkening the lower. He was still shamelessly comparing both my lipsticks when I entered.

Hector was on the edge of the bed with my shoulder bag at his feet and a book on his thigh, writing down the details of the return plane ticket I had been using to mark the page.

Miguel was studying Willow's driver's license.

I asked Ramiro, "Would you like to try on a dress?"

He turned from the mirror to peel back his lips for inspection, "Is it on my teeth?"

"No, but I still wouldn't go out looking like that."

Miguel picked Stephen Hawking's *Black Holes and Baby Universes* out of my bag and asked, "May I read?"

"Please, keep it."

"Thank you."

Then we all stood watching Hector take a third book out of the bag and pull out the perforated boarding pass I'd been using to hold another page. "A good flight?"

"Yes, thank you."

"And this is your address?" Miguel showed me the license then gave it to Hector to record all the information on it.

I asked, "What are y'all doing?"

Ramiro spread his arms and started to sing, "Getting to know you, getting to know all about you, getting to like you ..."

He was a loud baritone, and I had to strain to hear Miguel saying, "I will give to you something very important. I want to know ..." he gestured to Ramiro.

"... all about you."

Miguel held up two credit cards from my wallet. "Why is the name Laura Jackson?"

"She's my best friend. She let me use her cards for this trip."

"Why is she not here?"

"She had to work."

"Why you come alone? Why not wait?"

I looked away and grimaced, "It was a bad breakup. I needed to get away."

"With Laura?"

"No, another girl."

Miguel considered it before shaking his head and accepting, "Okay."

Pen in hand, ready to write, Hector asked, "Laura's address and phone number?"

"No," I was firm. "You don't get that."

"Is okay, guapa," Ramiro smiled two shades of wrong. "We no talk with Laura."

I hadn't pulled Laura out of the air with a forged birth certificate. She was real and living in Tennessee, unaware of what I was doing to her credit. That was going to be surprise enough. I didn't think she needed three angry Mexicans showing up at her door as well.

I said, "Maybe this is a bad idea."

"No, is okay. Laura is your ..." Ramiro searched for the word.

"She is our guarantee," Miguel corrected.

There were four Laura Jacksons in Tennessee at the time. One of them lived in Fayetteville, so I'd purposefully gone there to rent a house and connect a phone in a second Laura's name. I was trying to think out the ramifications of giving away my Laura's location while the Mexicans watched me, but I couldn't concentrate with them staring, so my reasoning went awry. I thought the double names in one city would confound them, like it had been confusing the creditors. I said, "Alright," and gave them the address of the rented house and the phone number with me on the answering machine saying, "This is Laura."

~~~~~~

The cocaine-filled statue of the Virgin Mary wasn't as I expected. It was ceramic, but that's where the similarity stopped. What was disconcerting was it was obviously empty. It was just a great big round clay pot with eyes, nostrils, and mouth. Both ugly and boring.

It was sitting on the coffee table and I was turning my head, studying it, hoping to make sense of it. "It's a …?"

"A monkey," Hector said.

"Oh." It was not obvious.

Four of us were staring at it and nobody looked impressed.

I was honest, "I really thought y'all were going to have me smuggle cocaine. I don't understand this."

Ramiro sighed. "Tampoco lo entiendo.

"We don't understand either," Miguel translated.

Ramiro might have been a better liar, but I believed him. I did not believe Miguel.

219

But I said, "Okay," and I meant it. I'd take this monkey through customs. "Where is it going?"

"My friend is called Tony. His address is Peachtree Street in Atlanta. I will tell you where and you will remember. You will not write it."

"Okay."

"Also, you will remember my phone number. You will call me when you give this to Tony."

"Okay."

Miguel and I looked at each other for several long moments until he finally asked, "You want money for this?"

I didn't mean to laugh, but I thought my lack of concern was rather transparent. "I suppose that would make it proper," then looking at the pot, "but I imagine you've already guessed, I'm not doing this for the money."

GIVE IT A NAME

I had three days before my flight returned home and I was spending them at the stucco house. The start of the first day, I ran my hand down the back of my thigh and felt a small circle of skin slide away. Tennessee is crawling with brown recluse spiders and one of the little rot-mouths had bitten me. The flesh was already decaying and it had the potential to get much worse, so I went to the doctor's and then to the pharmacy with a prescription for three antibiotics.

The pharmacist wanted to know what the cocktail was for because he didn't think he could fill it, so I explained about the spider and he came out to look at my leg. As he did, the teenage assistant behind the counter looked to see also and grimaced with disgust, then feigned a gag in his mouth. Moaning a warning, he tried to wave the pharmacist away.

The pharmacist said a few rough words to him and then apologized to me, saying, "He is a child, forgive him." He went on to explain, "I understand this spider venom. I will make for you the same medicine as for leprosy," and then left to prepare it.

Alright, sure, I wasn't going to argue because I didn't know a thing about it.

But the little shit behind the counter had a few opinions. He tutted, "Leprosy. Bad disease. I don't think you will have much luck at the clubs with leprosy." He sadly shook his head to emphasize my misfortune. Then he brightened to declare, "Would be better to have herpes."

Well, that was an opening I had never heard before. I was staring at him somewhat dumbfounded when he continued, "You Americans are *waa*," he cried, "about herpes, but is no big problem. I would have herpes to leprosy."

"Interesting choice," I couldn't quite bring myself to smile. "Given an option, I might have gone for something a little more exotic like rabies, or perhaps tetanus."

"No," he frowned at my selection. "Herpes is better. Better than AIDs. Much better than leprosy. Maybe you have herpes on your leg?"

"Maybe I do," I was starting to get the hang of this conversation. "Maybe you're right. I might prefer a couple of blisters to rotting flesh. In fact, I think I would."

"Yes, herpes is better than leprosy."

The discussion continued until I didn't know what I had on my leg but well understood Americans were entirely too uptight about herpes and he'd been spurned because of it. I apologized for the entire nation: "We are a bunch of assholes."

I walked out of the pharmacy shaking my head, thinking that was a conversation I would never revisit. I meant to file it somewhere under forget and then carry on with my spider bite as though it had never happened, but in a few days, it was going to unexpectedly find its way back into the in-box.

It wasn't anything I was going to share with Katia though. I was too much of an American to think you could say the word herpes around a lover and not lose them. And while I was keeping my mouth shut, I didn't mention leprosy or anything about a clay monkey pot either.

She had no idea why Miguel was sending us to the sprawling market to buy souvenirs, but he wanted my luggage to be packed with multiple crafts, especially Mayan trinkets, and anything antique, or clearly handmade.

Katia haggled, laughed, and occasionally cursed or stalked off knowing she'd be called back, and I stood aghast like a tourist, embarrassed she was arguing the price.

Back at the house, Ramiro was waiting to stuff the pot with trinkets encased in bubble wrap and then he swaddled the pot in more. It went into a transparent mesh bag like a ball, and Miguel said, "You will keep this …" he didn't know the word, so sat down to cradle it against his stomach. "Always here."

"In my lap, okay."

"Like a baby."

"Okay."

"Not up there," pointing overhead.

"Not in the compartment. I understand. In my lap. Like a baby." I was smiling indulgence.

Then with a little hug, Miguel repeated, "This is a baby."

~~~~~~

~~~~~~

Late on the second day, Miguel knocked on Katia's door to say, "We must talk."

While getting dressed to go downstairs, I rearranged my features to ensure I had the face of an innocent angel because I'd heard it in Miguel's voice, something was very wrong.

Hector was on one couch and Ramiro had flipped a dining room chair to straddle its back. It was already tense but Miguel made it worse by pacing. They appeared mostly confused, and I could see they wanted to be convinced all was good, but they were on the edge of anger and about to tip.

I said from behind the empty couch, "Tell me why you're upset."

Katia had arrived at the bottom of the stairs and Miguel pointed her into a chair against the wall saying, "Sit."

Then to me, "What is your name?"

Oh, wow, that was like getting slapped back to Dallas. Considering the question opens nearly every beginner's language course, it's surprising how rarely that exact sentence is actually spoken. I was pretty certain I hadn't heard it in eight years, but it was less the words than the tone that hurt me. It should have been expected considering the games I played, but it took me a moment to recover, and I hoped in the evening light, no one had seen my face flush.

I said, "You know my name, so tell me what is happening."

224

Miguel held up the license with Willow's name for me to see. "You said this is your home."

"Well," I conceded without showing guilt, "it is the old family home." It was the dilapidated ruin on the way to campus that I had first sent to Passport Services. I had used it again with Willow because I wanted to give her address meaning. I wanted to tie her name to the past, to the first laser printer and Mittwede and our races through the curves. But I was so familiar with the route, I'd stopped seeing it years before. If the house had been bulldozed, I might not have noticed.

"Do you live here?"

"I don't sleep there."

"You said to me you live here."

"It is my home. My permanent address. All my mail goes there. For simplicity, I tell people I live there." I was smiling, "Shall I assume you've sent someone around to knock on the door?"

Looking at the floor, Hector said three emotionless words in Spanish.

I could imagine what they were when Miguel accused, "There is no door."

I snapped, "Of course there's a door," but there probably wasn't. I had propped it up seven years before and suspected it had fallen back down. I should have known Miguel would not trust his baby to just a name on a license. Someone they knew in the States had obviously traveled to see the place, but it wasn't anyone in this room, and a house with no door it not the sort of thing to admit. "There has been no deception on my part. I told you I had just broken up with my girlfriend. You wanted to know my home address and you have it. You are holding it in your hand. The State would not have issued that license if that was not my home."

But Hector was talking to the floor again, flatly stating multiple facts unknown to me, and Miguel was trying to listen to us both.

When we were silent, he said, "Laura's house is also empty."

Well, hell. It was empty save for an answering machine. I hadn't even bothered to hang curtains, so it was a simple matter for anyone to see straight through the place.

Deny and concede had always been my most successful tactic. I said, "It's in a state of upheaval, but it's not empty. Laura and I are in the process of moving into an apartment together."

Miguel and Hector spoke together and in their words was a great deal of doubt.

Miguel held up Willow's license and said, "I think maybe this is not you."

"Seriously?" I laughed. "The picture isn't that bad. That is obviously me."

"This is nothing. I could have this made tonight."

"Dude, I have to go through US Immigration with that. Do you not think they can spot a fake? And if they have any misgivings, it's a simple phone call to Tennessee to confirm it's legitimate." Hands out to stop it going further, "Tell me what you need from me to make this right."

Miguel's emotions were running up and down the scale of trust and tripped on something close to hope, "Your address."

I made the fatalistically amused expression of *You're not going to like this*, and said, "It's in your hand," then pacifying, "I know, I know, but that really is the address that will always lead to me, and I knew you'd have issues if I told you I was moving into an apartment but don't know the address. It's in Lewisburg, which is Laura's hometown, and I'm not yet familiar with the city. Let me call her and I'll get the address."

I called the answering machine that had my voice saying "This is Laura," and had a "Please pick up" conversation with myself that went nowhere.

"Laura's house is empty," I was reminded.

First deny, "No, it's not," and then concede, "It may be in boxes, but she will be back tonight. I will call again later."

~~~~~~~

By midnight I was dragging tired and Laura still hadn't come home. The three guys had been doing lines of cocaine off the dining room table while I rested against the arm of the couch reading different books from my bag. The mood in the house had shot past paranoid hours before, but I was pretending not to notice the aggression. My flight was in twelve hours and Hector was angry they had run out of coke.

Miguel used the phone and then they started arguing amongst themselves.

They had told Katia to leave shortly after my first failed call and she'd wordlessly obeyed. Repeatedly I had wanted to offer that

227

we all shake hands and walk away, but every time I was about to say it, my head would explode with sirens, warning me it would be disastrous. It would look like I was backing away, defensive, in the wrong, and showing fear, but worse, it would force the issue of what they planned to do with me. Because they had to do something. And it was obvious from the start they weren't going to let me follow Katia out the door, so instead of bringing the situation into premature bargaining, I was waiting. I didn't know for what, not exactly, but I was looking for some sort of opening, an opportunity to turn it around or gracefully escape, but it was becoming apparent I had made a terrible mistake. Time had stretched things from bad into violent.

Hector threw a glass ashtray over my head into the stairs.

I didn't look up, just turned the page.

The volume of their fight escalated until Ramiro slammed Miguel against the wall while Hector shouted in his face.

I kept reading even though I was too alarmed to see the type.

Miguel shrugged Ramiro off and they all stood in angry conference, occasionally throwing an arm out in my direction.

The book became far more fascinating. Absolutely nothing was going to tear my attention from it.

Minutes passed before Miguel, then Hector, and finally Ramiro swiveled a chair away from the table to sit in a row and stare at me like a terrible problem they needed to solve.

I'd been on the same page for far too long but I didn't want to move, afraid the slightest action would trigger something awful.

Their dialogue was sporadic and irritated. They weren't comfortable in the straight backed chairs. One or the other would constantly be shifting, adjusting, huffing out aggravation, or falling forward to hang their arms between their knees and then back to flex their shoulders.

I knew the scene was about to break and I was dreading the change. Ramiro took a bottle from his shirt pocket and ate a pill. Miguel slapped his leg and Ramiro gave the bottle to him, and then Miguel handed the bottle to Hector.

All three had swallowed a pill and it gave Ramiro an idea. He gestured to me and Miguel agreed.

I was barely breathing, thinking, *Oh god, here we go.*

Miguel came to stand before me with his hand out and four blue pills in his palm. I looked up into his face when he said, "Have these," then over to Hector who was bringing a glass of rum and coke that had melted into two colors.

I sat up and asked, "Valium?"

Miguel nodded.

I gave a quiet laugh as though the idea were insane. "I can't take four. It's too much. I'll be asleep for twenty-four hours. No," I was shaking my head, "I'll miss my flight."

"I will wake you."

I didn't have to feign an expression of worry. I was certain they planned to kill me, thinking I would be too drugged to fight. And I didn't want them to suspect one, four, or twelve was all the same to me. I said, "One is plenty."

Miguel pushed the lot on me saying, "Four."

"How about just two?"

"Four," he insisted.

I said, "I swear, you really do have my address."

"Is okay, guapa," Ramiro was still at the table. "You sleep. Fly home tomorrow."

I pulled at Miguel's wrist, saying, "Please sit," until he was on the edge of the coffee table. "This is truly not necessary. We are both aware the plan is not going forward. It is fine. I am no more trouble for you than before we met. I will leave ..."

"You will stay."

"Or stay. Okay. But this," I was trying to close his hand on the pills, "is really not required."

Hector said, "I promise, no bad thing will happen."

I shook my head to refuse and Miguel leaned closer to warn, "I will make you."

That was a humiliation I did not want to experience. I could clearly imagine the struggle, and after a brawl like that, none of us would be able to pretend anything was going to get better. I accepted the pills saying, "I suppose I won't be too concerned about it in a moment anyway."

~~~~~~

The last time I had taken anywhere near 40 mgs of diazepam I had taken 50 with Mittwede. He had wanted to prove he could get me wasted. I was trying to remember how he had acted on a similar dose. I couldn't recall anything except he had done it again without me and slept right through the fire that killed him.

And then there was the Vietnam vet at the country club. We'd gone pill for pill, four colors and eight shapes, until he was slinking down the wall to the pro-shop. I had meant to drive him home but he'd wrapped his truck around a telephone pole before I knew he was gone.

There was a near legendary misconception that I was tough when I was really just unaffected. For whatever reason, the receptors in my brain didn't accept pharmaceuticals. While everyone else drooled into the furniture, I'd be straight up sober and most often annoyed to be denied such obvious pleasure. But now with my head against the arm of the couch, I was thinking this mental glitch was the only thing that was going to save me. I was convinced the men would strangle me.

Twenty silent minutes in and I didn't know if I was affecting drowsiness too soon. I wondered how long I should wait before feigning sleep.

I listened to Ramiro in the kitchen cooking and heard Hector go up the stairs. Miguel was on the opposite couch, watching when I closed my eyes and said with detached calm, "It would be great if you didn't kill me. I'd really appreciate it. But if you do, you have my address. Please let my mother know. They say the uncertainty is the worst part."

"Okay, turista."

That was not what I wanted to hear. I was hoping for strong denials and pleasant assurances, but I showed no distress, merely gave a faint smile like I had received them and played like I was slipping away.

Shortly after, there was a knock at the door and a boisterous man entered. I didn't stir but Miguel was off the couch and Hector was coming fast down the stairs. Everyone was greeting and laughing, and my heart was pounding, terrified this was the person who was going to dump my body in the jungle.

But instead, Miguel and Hector left with him, and Ramiro came to eat on the opposite couch. I heard him flicking through the first pages of a book. He said, "Hi, Willow. How are you? Good, thanks. How are you?"

Then, a few bites of food and the page turned.

"Where do you live, Ms. Willow? In a house? With no door? How wonderful!"

Once I figured out he had a phrasebook and was practicing English on me, I had to bite the inside of my cheeks not to smile. It became a struggle.

"Would you like to go on a date with me? Would you like to have dinner with me? I know a good Chinese Italian restaurant. Waiter, waitress a table for two please. I have a reservation."

I had to groan and bury my face like a disturbed sleeper because my lips were curling against my will.

He ate and flipped the pages.

"I like you. Do you like me?" His voice lost the singsong tone to drop dramatically low, "Your eyes say yes." Then back to the phrasebook, "We are having a good time. May I hold your hand? Would you mind if I kissed you?"

He was quiet, seemed to be considering it, and I was wondering if I was about to be molested.

"Guapa, I like you, but you a little loco, no?" He smacked his lips against the air and carried on. "Thank you. That was a very nice kiss."

Before he was done, we had taken a train trip, rented a hotel with a Jacuzzi, and gone shopping for baseball caps. He flipped through the pages to conclude, "Thank you, Willow, this has been fun. Can we do it again sometime? May I have your phone number?" Rising from the couch, he returned to his own voice to say, "No. Willow no give phone number," then walked over to thump me on the head with the book. "Willow no give address," thwacked again. "Willow no give nada," double whack before he climbed the stairs.

FOREIGN ROADS

With the amount of diazepam in me, I should have been content to lie back and let events unfold as they may, and my curiosity did for a moment consider it, but then a punch of panic reminded me that people far saner than I were murdered for less in more conspicuous locations.

I was hyper alert for the sound of Ramiro, but the stucco house had concrete floors and they don't creak like wood. He was up the stairs but I had no idea where. I was debating with myself if I should wait, perhaps to hear the sound of the shower or something to indicate he would be gone long enough for me to get to the door, and then enough time passed that I could have been gone. I shouldn't have hesitated. The next instant I was off the couch, sweeping up my bag of books and heading for the exit. I stopped at the breakfast bar to search its random clutter for my return ticket. My hands were stiff and my brain was screaming, "Run," but I was talking to myself, saying, "Calm, calm, you have handled worse," ignoring the mental return demanding, "When? Tell me when?"

I was pretty certain it was the most terrified I had ever been. Expected disaster was so much worse than being in the center of it. The fear of being caught off the couch, walking around perfectly lucid, was near enough to ensure I would pass out if anyone saw me.

"Mumble inanities and pretend you're sleep-walking," I told myself, just strolling around with a bag of books.

From the spread of litter on the bar, I reclaimed Willow's license, and while I was there, I plucked a set of car keys from a bowl of change, and then, fuck it, no reason not to sling the mesh bag with the monkey pot over my shoulder as well, because, *why not?* Running this close to the cliffs, the allure of throwing myself over was too strong to resist.

I couldn't find my return ticket, and my carry-on was upstairs. Neither mattered though. My wallet with credit cards was still in my shoulder bag and I had enough cash to see me clear of Mexico.

By the front door, I slipped into my shoes and then went for the lock. The bolt turning on the door was silent, but the door opening seemed to suck sound through the house. I pulled it to the frame but left it unlatched. The keys in my hand were dirty and worn with a Volkswagen emblem, and the pergola across the street held Miguel's Mercedes and a pale blue Carmen Ghia with an orange hood.

Throwing the bag of books onto the VW's floor and the baby into the passenger seat, I stepped one foot forward to the Mercedes, thinking I needed to sabotage it, but my mind was screaming, "There isn't time," so stepped back; then spun forward and back a few more times until I was motion sick and about to hurl. Every sound in the street was Ramiro in pursuit and I didn't want to be killed, but I also did not want to be chased in a Volkswagen by a Mercedes.

"You are a goddamn professional," I mentally slapped myself and went forward. It was too dark to see under the shelter so I brushed my fingers over the Mercedes' body until I was at the rear fender. Kneeling at the tire, I searched for the screw cap and threw it aside to shove the engine key at the invisible pin, then went wide-eyed horrified at the sound. Air escaping from the valve filled the street and an American on an unlit boat at the dock was shouting, "Hey, what are you doing?"

I called back from the pitch black, "It's cool. We're going off road and there's too much pressure in the tires." I stopped and ran my hand over the gravel at my feet, trying to make it sound like I was moving to another tire. "Thanks man, it's great people are watching out."

"Is that your car?"

Air was hissing loud into the night again, "Well hell, I hope so, or someone's going to be pissed."

"That's a lot of air you're letting out."

"Four tires is a lot of air," I explained. Running my hand over the gravel again, I waited a few seconds before depressing the pin again. "You should have seen us earlier tonight. We got drunk and over filled them to see if they would pop. Rental cars, man, no one's kind to a rental." Then it was flat, and I was hurrying for the Volkswagen asking, "Going to get ice for the cooler. You need anything?"

"Uh, no … but thanks."

As if all of that was not enough to alert Ramiro, the turning of the Carmen Ghia's engine was a stuttering trick of gas, clutch, and pleading sweet-talk. I drove down the street with my hands too tight on the steering wheel, aware the street was narrow enough to block me in if I crossed paths with Miguel and Hector.

Turning onto the main tourist strip was just another worry. Boulevard Kukulkan is long. Incredibly long. Like thirty mind-rending, neverending miles long, and if you happen to turn the wrong way when you first enter, it's even longer. I'd seen quite a few VW Beetles but not another Carmen Ghia, and I suspected Cancun only had one that was blue with a vivid off-color orange hood. I felt like I was making a touring spectacle of my escape.

When I got myself oriented correctly, I was heading out of town, away from the tourist hotels, the bars, and the beach, following the occasional sign for the airport and the ruins in the jungle. There was a wide median with intermittent palm trees and foliage that separated the two lanes. It did nothing to hide the car but went a long way in obscuring both me and the occupants of the passing vehicles.

It was unnerving. I felt certain I would encounter Miguel and Hector, either in a car beside me or passing back to the coast and the stucco house. I wanted fully out of Cancun. My plan was to drive to the next largest city and arrange a flight home from there, but where that city was, I had no idea. The road signs were inexplicable. I knew about the Mayan ruin, Chichen Itza, so at first I was following those signs, but they seemed to wrap back into Cancun. I thought I was driving in circles so I started following the signs to Merida. The route led straight through the city until the median grew thin and the street lights few.

I had finally convinced myself I was safe, thinking I had traveled far enough away from the city hub, and deep enough into the undeveloped outskirts, that the chances of passing the rich Mexicans were low. I was out in scrub brush and squat cement buildings that looked like workshops and garages, but it was there, right on the edge of town that a passing car slammed on the breaks and swung around to follow.

~~~~~

It had happened too fast for me to recognize what type of car had turned to pursue, and in the rearview mirror it was nothing but alternating high and low headlights. I couldn't imagine why they bothered. It wasn't like I was going to pull over.

I had the speedometer needle buried past 140, but I knew I wasn't going anywhere near a hundred and already the car wasn't steady.

I reminded myself, "I love to be chased. I absolutely love to be chased."

This wasn't my first car chase. I'd had another a couple months before, though at markedly lower speeds. Absurd really for how harrowing it was when we never reached 40.

It was on the night of the ice storm and I'd just cleared out the company safe. For a decade, you could mention it to anyone in Tennessee as the Ice Storm and everyone would remember the night with awe. It started out weird because it was February and an approaching storm had pushed the temperature close to seventy, but as the clouds neared, the mercury started to drop and it kept falling through the day. The sky was dark purple and gothic before evening, and the temperature kept plummeting, turning the clouds wild, threatening tornadoes, and soon the thermometers read freezing but it was still getting colder. Then it was dark and the rains started. By

7:00 p.m. it was splashing across the pavement as frozen slush, covering everything in rippling cables of ice. It was stunning but extremely dangerous.

No one should have been out in it, but I was a couple of hours from home in Columbia, trying to break into a floor safe. The idea came from a book I'd read a decade before, and while I couldn't remember the title, I never forgot the plot. The woman in it crossed the country accepting jobs as a secretary strictly to empty the vault. The book made it sound positively thrilling and left me wondering why more people didn't do it.

While I was experimenting with every other conceivable crime of identity, I figured I might as well test out that one as well. But I knew most firms didn't keep tens of thousands in the safe for secretaries to steal. I knew who did though: fast food. TCBY had taught me that. It was nowhere near as glamorous as the book, but I took a job at the Columbia Subway for three days. I had accepted the job on Tuesday and was taking advantage of the storm on Saturday.

At twenty-three, I was the oldest of four in the store and ordered everyone home for their own safety. I was demanding they leave, insisting I was fine, assuring I'd be right behind them. Then once alone, I fussed with the safe while the phone rang and rang. I knew it was the owner. I was moving fast to get the money and wipe away any traces of my fingerprints, and then the phone stopped ringing. The owner was coming. I knew he was because no one had answered the phone and official closing was still hours away.

The freezing rains had been coming down for close to an hour and it wasn't letting up. I left the front door unlocked to enter the storm.

It was brutal. Ice was cutting into my eyes, stinging the skin on my face and collecting in my hair. I'd parked two storefronts away in the Kroger parking lot and skated to my car. Slamming against the trunk, I was slipping to the door when the Subway owner skidded his truck to an uncertain stop before the store. I was trying to force my key into the frozen lock but my car was a block of ice, the doors frozen shut, the windscreen thick and opaque.

Freaking out, I slid into the grocery store to ask for help, certain the owner had seen me and would be out any second to confront me for the empty safe.

Two Kroger employees came out with a can of deicer and a scraper to hack their way into my car. As soon as the door was free, I turned the engine over and they worked on the windshield. But behind us, the owner was holding open Subway's door, looking at us, calling, then trying to race forward but sliding, falling, and crawling on his knees. I told the guys, "Enough, enough, that's great," but they had only managed to scrap a four-inch swatch in the windshield.

They said, "No, wait, you can't drive like this," but I had gently put the car in drive and was closing the door, saying, "No, really, thanks, it's great, really good," sliding forward as they skated back and then careened for the parking lot exit.

The owner was one of those good ol' boys that went out on nights like this to pull people out of ditches. His truck was normally capable but this night was extreme. More extreme than anyone could

240

remember and he wasn't having too easy of a time even getting into his ride.

At 5 mph, I made my blind escape. There wasn't much to see through the small opening and the sleet was covering it back up. On the road, I cut my lights and tried to turn right onto a side street but the tires started sliding. I was forced to turn the wheel to recover and coasted forward, past the escape and then noticed my encrusted back window was illuminated by headlights in the distance.

To the left were businesses but no streets that led away, and the lights from behind were getting brighter. I didn't want to trap myself but I could barely see and the next street turning right was far ahead while to the left was a gravel drive leading behind a brick building. There was nothing to do but follow it and hide.

Heater on max, I waited until defrost cleared my windshield, aware the owner's truck was making repeated passes, scouting the street, trying to find me. He had seen me turn but he didn't know exactly where.

And I was afraid to stay, certain he'd eventually become more committed and start exploring. Once he saw my exhaust, I'd be done. I waited until his lights swept by again and then crept onto the street, driving 10 mph but slipping every few seconds, unable to secure traction. The streets were empty, the town dead. Ice had encased absolutely everything. I was gliding through a residential area watching limbs from overhead trees fall through the power lines and shatter against the street. It was too treacherous to swerve so I was driving over them.

It had taken ages, but I was two blocks away with a branch sticking out of my grill. I thought I had lost the Subway owner, but then, sliding through a four-way intersection, no way to stop, I looked left into his face for slow motion recognition.

Now he was behind me. I pushed it to 20 but he was gaining. Sleet and slush and rain were coming down together and he was driving too fast for the conditions. He started spinning out, headlights whipping right and then left across my mirrors.

He slid off the road into a ditch and I was glad to be escaping. But he had four-wheel drive and was quickly out of the gutter and back on the road. He was more cautious but he was still coming. Through the city we sped at school zone speeds, first one then the other swerving wildly across the road, sliding wide on the turns, me fleeing, him pursuing.

On the highway, I thought I was being suicidal going 30 but I needed distance between us, and he must have thought he could hang back and catch me when I inevitably ditched.

For an hour we sped recklessly through the storm, dropping to 10, racing to 35, but never higher, my headlights off, his on high, both of us losing control when we tried to go faster. I had put a fair space between us when he suddenly started gaining, and then abruptly and finally his lights arced sideways and he was gone from my rearview mirror.

It had been an absurd low-speed chase.

Now in Mexico, I was going 140 kilometers per hour, no idea what it meant in miles except the needle could no longer register an increase in speed. The car was shaking and the tires were light on the road, and that was never good.

I had once been told, "Everybody thinks they're a good driver."

Well, I had no such illusions. I was a shockingly bad driver. I was pretty certain I held a gold standard of incompetence that no one would dispute.

But I excelled at wrecking. I was a freaking genius when it came to crashing a car.

By the time I took possession of the Carmen Ghia, I had *un*intentionally totaled a dozen cars and mangled a few more. I was an appalling driver that no one dared ride with twice, but in those wild, screaming we're-all-going-to-die moments of an accident, when it was all throwing down and turning over, I was a Zen master. I'd had so many wrecks, I could see clearly where a crash was going and would often avoid the worst of it by accelerating. I thought I held a PhD in Unexpected Automobile Demolition.

As such, I could just sit in a car and know exactly how it would fair in a collision. And I did not want to drive the Carmen Ghia into anything stronger than a scrub brush. At whatever unknown speeds we were reaching, if the Volkswagen collided with something, it would crumple and I'd be wrapped up in it.

But I couldn't slow down because Miguel and Hector were following. There was no other explanation for the lunacy of this chase.

We had sped through the outskirts of Cancun and were now about thirty miles away, passing through sporadic jungle, scrub, and then random roadside businesses in low cement buildings. The high and low beams were still flashing up and down in the mirrors, and the effect was approaching something close to a strobe light as the car shook against the speed.

Various road signs whizzed by but I had no idea what they meant. The warning of *tope* would have meant nothing to me even if I had seen it, but I didn't think there was any advance warning. The thing was stretched across the road and beside it was a sign with an arrow pointing down at it, declaring: *Tope*. There it is. Two twelve-inch speed bumps laid down right in the middle of the open highway, one after the other, and my speedometer was maxed-out buried.

I knew the car following had hit the brakes, and that probably should have told me something, but I was driving fast to put space between us and they were dropping away.

I was watching the distance expand in the rearview mirror, feeling pretty good about things, then *wham!*, my hands were off the steering wheel and I was on my back, staring straight up into black.

For the briefest moment, I lost all sense of what was happening. It wouldn't have surprised me to look over and see Ed sleeping in our bed. I had no idea of anything much less that I was in Mexico, in a stolen car, driving through the jungle with lunatics in pursuit. Then it all came back with the sound of a vehicle losing control in the gravel. I knew the sound well.

I had regained enough of my wits to know the car was speeding forward, ripping through the rocks on the shoulder and about to go wildly off road. Struggling against momentum, I was trying to rise up from the broken seat to grab the wheel while also feeling my foot across the pedals for the brake. Adding to the pandemonium, the driver's door was swinging free, escalating the sound and throwing dust into my eyes.

I'd never had a wreck like this: one I couldn't see. But I couldn't get up to take control of the wheel because the car was bouncing over uneven terrain, slamming me back into the flattened seat, jarring loose everything the *tope* hadn't broken. The transmission was in fourth, and I had just found the brake when the car plowed into something dense that yielded and caught under the tires. The car stopped and the engine stalled.

I was still on my back, watching a tire ricochet off a roof and then bound back for the windshield. It filled me with dread but I couldn't look away. I was thinking, *This is going to hurt.* But the trajectory was high and it slammed off the roof, then shot off down the road.

I looked up to the rearview mirror, but the mirror was gone. The tire I could hear bouncing down the road and with it two doors opening. The pursuing car's headlights were steady on high now, illuminating the interior, and I was looking over into the passenger seat for anything I might be able to use as a weapon. The glove box was open and had thrown papers across the empty seat but it offered nothing. Dazed and a little weak, I was rolling for the ground outside the driver's door, thinking if nothing else, I would be shot defending myself with a stick.

But I was moving slow, so before I could get my legs to follow my face, there were feet outside the driver's door. I was looking down into delicate toes in feminine sandals and behind them another woman was streaming Spanish outrage.

She pushed past her quiet friend to reach into the car and begin a detailed list of everything that had fallen to the *tope*. Yanking the driver's seat up, she let it drop to show it was past repair and then cussed me out. She stretched across my lap, knocking me flat again, to flap the glove box door against its broken latch, and then cuss me some more. Slamming closed the driver's door, she pointed out it wouldn't catch either and then really let me have it. I imagine the next bit was all about the mirrors because the door had lost one and the rearview was somewhere on the dark floorboard with the baby.

I was staggering out of the wreck explaining, "It's okay, this is how I always park." But my exit just let her demand the location of the lost hubcap.

I had plowed into a massive stack of tires which collapsed across the hood and hid the broken headlight but not the dent in the roof. The concave pushed her to a new extreme. Of all the words chasing each other out of her mouth, I understood only two: "Ramiro," who I assumed knew these ladies, and "Puta," which I assumed was me.

There's only one way to deal with people like this: escalate.

I went full-scale American nuclear. I was taller than her and I was louder than her, and by the time I chased them back to their car, I was angrier. I was also shouting five words she understood: Miguel, Hector, and Ramiro, you fucking bitch.

~~~~~

~~~~~~

It wasn't like that crazy woman wasn't going straight to Ramiro for an explanation anyway. I hoped Candy and Bunny weren't around, because she sounded like a girlfriend. Maybe even a girlfriend that had let Ramiro borrow her car.

The distance put me a good hour ahead, but that didn't make me safe. I knew I could make that Mercedes do an easy 140 miles per hour, and if I were pressed, because someone had just abducted my monkey baby, I'd push German engineering close to flight.

They had the biggest advantage of knowing the road and I couldn't guess how many more of those damn invisible speed bumps were going to be spread across the highway.

I learned about *topes* like a laboratory rat learns not to touch the red button.

The Carmen Ghia backed out of the tires and impressed me by holding herself together, but she was a mess. I jammed a piece of roadside wood under the driver's seat to hold it upright, and then used the strap on my shoulder bag to tie the driver's door closed.

One light shining through the dark jungle night, I tried to figure out the symbol for impending chaos. I was super aware of every sign and mark on the road, but it still took a while to learn. At first I thought it was the white zebra lines painted on the asphalt that predicted my teeth were going to be scattered across the dash, but I'd stomp on the brake and no speed bump would appear. Then I'd head slam into one doing 100, certain there had been no suggestion whatsoever that it was there. For a while I thought it was the pedestrian-crossing sign, but that wasn't a consistent indicator for the brutality either.

Finally, an hour outside Merida, I made the association between the word *tope* and smashing havoc. It was a pretty innocuous looking word that at least deserved an exclamation point.

I'd had the Carmen Ghia for less than four hours but by the time I entered Merida, it looked like something from a demolition yard. The second *tope* had smashed the driver's window into little granules of glass, and I hadn't noticed which *tope* broke the emergency brake so that it lay limp in the cradle. It still had one hub cab but I'd had to stop to take the shoulder strap off the door because it was more important to tie down the hood, so the last hour had been particularly jarring.

My body felt as mistreated as the car, and I was shaking with fatigue. I was looking for the airport but was utterly lost. Whenever I saw a food vendor or little shop, I would stop to ask for directions but I was mangling that too.

I couldn't remember how I knew the phrase, but I was certain the way to ask if someone spoke English was "¿Hablo Ingles?" There was absolutely no doubt in my mind that this was correct. So, I spent several hours in Merida confidently walking up to strangers and inquiring, "Do I speak English?" and then not liking how the dialogue proceeded.

At wits end, I had the conversation again. I had stopped at a road side stall to ask a teenage boy and girl, "¿Hablo Ingles?"

They looked at each other and then stared at me. I asked again, "¿Hablo Ingles?"

The boy turned his head and ventured a somewhat stressed, "Es posible."

Trying to limit the available responses, I asked, "¿Hablo Ingles? Sí or no?"

He took an uncertain stab at it, "Sí."

I rambled out, "I'm sorry to bother you, but I am lost and need to know where the airport is."

But they just returned expressions of incomprehension, so I demanded with irritation, "¿Hablo Ingles?"

Now it seemed like I was issuing a strange test, and they both studied me for the answer. The boy was none too certain but raised his brows to guess, "¿Sí?"

I started in again, "I just need to know where the airport is. The airport? With the planes? Where is it?"

They were starting to look alarmed and I didn't know why they were toying with me. I was angry, snapping harshly, "¿Hablo Ingles?"

With perfect conviction this time, the boy was emphatic, "Sí."

The girl agreed, "Sí, hable Ingles."

"Then will you kindly speak it?"

Confusion as they turned their heads for understanding.

Blessed hell, why did every one say they spoke English when they didn't?

I drove around Merida making an ever-increasing ass of myself until inadvertently seeing a sign for the airport.

I needed rest but there was a flight into Mexico City in an hour and I wasn't lingering to have Miguel, Hector, or Ramiro catch me. I

249

couldn't sleep sitting upright, so I'd been awake for thirty-six hours when I arranged the next flight from Mexico City into Dallas. And that flight had been full, too, so I hit US Immigration and Customs like I'd just taken four blue pills of stupid.

MEXICAN POT

I was a single woman traveling alone out of Mexico City with nothing more than a shoulder bag of books and an ugly terracotta pot. It was not an ideal way to approach US Customs. Single women traveling unaccompanied are marked as drug mules. I knew this because I had been pulled aside countless times and told this by uniformed agents. They were always openly confounded as to why I was traveling alone when I clearly had no drugs.

The ball of bubble wrap was going to be suspect, and I had a different opinion than Miguel about how to smuggle. I had no experience with smuggling, but I was quite familiar with concealing things: You either buried it or hid it right out in the open.

I unwrapped the pot on the flight into Dallas and then spent exactly ten seconds on the rest of my plan.

I already had the problem of being a woman traveling alone, but not even a man could expect to walk unquestioned through US Customs without luggage. Because it was unusual, it was going to cause issues. But my ten-second plan was to handle it with a little innuendo about the pot. Perhaps it would go along the lines of, "Who needs luggage when you've got pot?" Then I'd turn on the charm and win the agents back.

I'd probably explain my lack of packed clothes with a bit of truth from another occasion, pulling on the time I had left all my dresses and cosmetics with a less fortunate friend. But I didn't really think any of this out. I didn't practice any part of the exchange in my head because I intended to play it like I always did, all on impulse, fresh in the moment. I'd zing out something provocative, and then sweet-talk my way clear of trouble.

But I'd lost my fresh, clean charm sometime in the previous night. I was approaching 48 hours awake and was having a hard time exchanging basic pleasantries.

I exited the plane without even glancing at the baggage turnstile and approached Customs with the bag of books over one shoulder and the pot under my arm.

The agent held me back saying, "You need to wait for your bags."

"It's fine. I don't have any."

He didn't think I understood. He stressed it with irritation, "You have to wait for your luggage before you can proceed into Customs."

"I have no luggage."

He pulled back with a scowl. "You don't have any luggage?"

"No."

"Ma'am, why don't you have any luggage?"

"Because I left all my marijuana at home." I'd been waiting to make my pot joke and there it was, funny as a guillotine. I quickly tried to put my head back on. "No. No, that's not it. I actually brought my marijuana," and put forward the monkey pot. "No, that's not it either," and pulled it back. "It's pot," that was the joke, "I have a lot of pot. No, wait, that's not right either."

252

"Ma'am, will you step over here?" Into that special place where the agents congregate with seam rippers and gloves. The three agents who had been watching were now beside him. He asked, "You want to explain again why you have no luggage?"

"I don't need clothes."

"I think you do, ma'am."

"Not like others do."

"Others?"

"Mmm," I agreed.

"Others, like me?"

"Well, if I had another dress you could have it."

"I don't need a dress, ma'am."

"It's okay. I don't mind. I left my lipsticks with a man." I was so fuck-ton tired, I could not claw my way into making sense.

The agent squeezed his eyes to become a mind reader. He guessed, "Did you leave your clothes with someone else?"

"Yes. *Thank you*," for getting that out of my head.

"Oh. Kay. Moving on." Motioning for my shoulder bag, he looked inside at the three remaining books. He asked, "Are you carrying any drugs or weapons?"

"Drugs, yes, drugs, I have drugs."

All the agents widened their eyes and nodded at my enthusiastic reply. One said to the others, "I'd have never guessed she was carrying drugs."

My agent asked, "Would you like to tell me where?"

"In the zipper."

Opening the internal pocket, he held up the prescription bottle. "What is this for?"

"Herpes. No. Leprosy."

Fingers splayed wide, the bottle was dropped and he was firm, "Ma'am, you can go."

I opened my mouth to speak, but he stepped back and pointed to the glass doors, "Go."

I could have had three pounds of cocaine in the monkey, but he didn't care. He didn't look. Didn't want to look. Didn't want to exchange one more word with me.

~~~~~~

The second Laura Jackson in Fayetteville got a strange call from a payphone in Texas. "Hi, Laura, this isn't going to make any sense, and I can't explain it right now, but if unknown Mexicans come to your house, you might want to call the cops. It could get violent. They may want to kill you."

"Uh, do I know you? Who is this?"

"I know this sounds like a crank call, but I'm quite serious. Mexicans: Bad. I intend to fix it, but for the next few days …"

"*Mexicans*? I don't like being threatened. Who is this?"

"Laura, you're having an adventure. You didn't ask to come along, but here you are. There's nothing you can do about it at this point except catch up with the plot. There are some Mexicans that think you're a lesbian… Well, no, wait, I never actually said you were into women."

"This is *not* funny."

"I said it was an adventure, not a comedy. Now listen, you need to be careful. Lock the doors, load the gun, and be prepared to call the cops. Maybe you should just go away for a few days."

"Are you being serious?"

"Well," I wish I weren't, but, "yes, and I am *so* sorry. I'm really much smarter than this, but I wasn't thinking straight. I swear, I'll have it sorted by the end of the week. Until then, remember: Mexicans want to kill you."

THE DEVIL'S FORKED TONGUE

Ed asked, "Where were you?"

And I said, "Home."

"I called every day of the week but you never answered."

"Oh, sorry, I turned the ringer off."

"Why?"

"I didn't want to be woken up and then I forgot to turn it back on."

He rolled his eyes at my absentmindedness and asked, "Where did you get all these bruises?"

Remembering another accident from months before, I laughed, "I was picking flowers on the side of the road and fell down the embankment."

"You are so clumsy. Are you alright?"

"Perfectly fine."

The monkey pot was on the top of the liquor cabinet in the living room. Ed looked at its wide eyes, flared nostrils, and oval mouth. He said, "I see Shawn gave you one of his pots."

"Mmm," I agreed.

Shawn was an archeologist that made pots that worried his colleagues. They thought his work could pass as genuine Mayan artifacts and didn't want them out in circulation. For fun, Shawn had aged a couple of his creations, and while it brought an appreciative grin to his face, it served only to further stress his associates.

I preferred Shawn's work, but I saw the similarity.

He could have identified the pot, but I tried to protect Ed and our dearest friends from having to make unpleasant ethical decisions. And I didn't want to wrestle Shawn over a monkey when I had Laura to worry about.

And besides, the pot's identity was not as interesting to me as getting it to Tony in Atlanta. The Cancun boys would never expect it. The act would leave them mystified for the rest of their lives, and I'd get to spend the rest of mine imagining their befuddlement every time they thought of Willow.

~~~~~~

Peachtree Street sounds lovely but I was in an ugly block of brick and concrete offices. Tony was a financial advisor in one of them and his beautiful secretary didn't like the look of me. "He won't see you. He's not expecting you."

"You've made it more than clear he is a busy man, but if you'd just kindly tell him I have come with a monkey, we'll let him decide if he has the time."

She looked at the ball of bubble wrap in my arms and thought less of it than me. Getting to her feet, her smile was forced and her words were sharp with disdain, "Tony is not in the monkey business."

I couldn't believe she had actually said it. A person could spend their whole life looking for the opportunity to make that joke, and anyone with a middling of self-respect would still back away from it. I had to ask, "Was that your attempt at a witticism?"

But she wasn't turning around. She slipped into his office with the door tight around her body lest I see him.

And then moments later, she was leaving and Tony's voice was loud and defensive, "I don't know what she's on about but I want you to send her in here."

I made a quick review of where I was because if I were at the wrong place, this could get odd.

The secretary wouldn't even look at me, but the way was clear so I walked through. Tony was standing behind the desk with a red angry face which was made vivid against his pink shirt and tie. He was a big ol' man that looked on the verge of a heart attack, and he needed to wheeze a breath before bellowing at me, "Shut the door young lady and explain what this is about."

I was more convinced I had come to the wrong place and started forming a story about a monkey wrench. It was all going to be a misunderstanding about a borrowed tool.

But when I turned around from the closed door, he was smiling excited, asking in a whisper, "Is that the monkey head vase?"

"I'm glad you were expecting it."

"I wasn't. No one told me you were coming. Let me see it," and he was out from behind his desk, hands outstretched to take it.

His fingers were too pudgy to get a proper grip on the tape, so I came tentatively forward offering, "Wait, here, let me," and laid it bare on his desk.

The only time I had ever looked as enthralled as he did, I was holding the velvet muzzle of a white race horse named Tanya.

The terracotta pot on the desk left me cold, but Tony had a fever for it that made his breath rasp harder than before.

I just couldn't see it.

I wanted to see it though. I stood motionless studying it until he mistook my waiting as a signal for payment.

"I wasn't told to expect you. I don't know what agreement was made for your delivery fee."

I was at a loss. I couldn't think of a thing he might have that I would want. I said, "Tell me something unusual."

"What?"

"Tell me something that will shock me. That's all. A perfect payment: Shock me."

"Are you serious?"

"Would you prefer I ask for cash?"

"I don't know. Maybe. You're weird, aren't you? You don't look it. But you are. Aren't you?"

"By most standards, yes. But maybe you're weirder?"

"I fucked a cow once."

"No, that's not good enough. I've heard that one before."

"Alright." He was thinking, looking through the solid wall at the place his secretary sat.

I stopped him, "I've probably heard that one, too. I'm going to need you to think beyond the flesh."

"Okay, I've got something for you. It has to do with the flesh, but not, you know …" he pointed at his pants.

I nodded.

Pulling his brows together, he went looking for the memory and the way to say it. I had been hoping for something vaguely funny, but I could see from his expression that wasn't the direction we were going. "I have never told this to anyone."

I nodded again and waited solemnly.

He appeared a little nauseous and had to swallow. "I was raised by a real son-of-a-bitch. Not my daddy but his. A real piece of work, hand-carved by the devil out of spite. He'd take a belt or a switch to anything he could catch. Thought the whole world was going to hell and he alone stood between it and damnation. He'd beat me for no reason except it was Sunday, always telling me, 'Those with a forked tongue go to the devil.'"

So far his story was much the same as I'd heard countless times before. Brutal child abuse was common in the South, spanning generations so that it seemed everyone I knew had either been whipped with a belt or beaten with a hair brush. My sister and I were the exception. From a very early age, I knew my parent's Northern sanity was something to be cherished.

But Tony didn't have such luck. His accent was Old South. He said of his grandfather, "Bastard always thought I was lying, and if my memaw tried to defend me, he thought she was lying, too, so he'd beat us both. Well, that old bastard died of a stroke. I can't say that I was sad except to see memaw cry. She was a true Christian. She was an angel. When it was her turn, she'd be going to heaven. And I wasn't going to have that bastard up there with her."

Seemed reasonable to me, so I smiled encouragement.

"'Those with a forked tongue go to the devil,' that's what he always said. He was laid out all proper at the funeral home and I came prepared. I had a carpet cutter and a pair of pliers and I was going to send him to hell."

I didn't so much laugh as have all the air constricted out of me by surprise.

Seeing that I understood, Tony nodded, "Yeah. But I thought his mouth would just pop open and I'd pull his tongue out easy as pie. But his lips were sealed. Just clamped tight. Fighting me, I thought. Then I saw the stitches. Someone had sewn his mouth shut. Probably to keep the bastard from speaking while they dressed his sorry ass. So, I was using the carpet cutter to get in there, and I was making a hell of a mess. Just sliced his lips from one side to the other and still didn't get those stitches. So I had to go at it again."

My own mouth was open and my eyes were wide.

"Every cut I made just opened his lips up like a flower spreading its petals. And then bits started coming loose. I tried to hold them in place but by the time I got his mouth open, I'd near enough removed all his lips. *Hoowee*, I tell you, it was a sight."

I nodded, imagining it would have been.

"I got his tongue out and forked it down the middle as I intended, but it wasn't going back in. It was just sort of sticking up out of... It was all," Tony waggled his fingers over his mouth, "all bare teeth. Didn't have any lips."

I grimaced understanding.

"Aw buddy, I tell you, I started panicking. I was trying to shove it back into his mouth but his jaw just opened wider and the tongue wasn't going away. And like right then, just all of a sudden, I saw him. What he looked like. No lips and all teeth and forked tongue. Flipped me straight out. I started crying and ran into the parking lot to hide."

Now he was quiet so I had to ask, "And then? I mean... who found him?"

"I don't know," he sounded haunted. "I didn't go back in there."

Now I did laugh.

"Do you think I'm going to hell for that?"

I laughed again. "No, you're not going to hell for that." And when he looked doubtful, "I promise, that is not hell worthy," but I was only trying to make him feel better.

"Was that shocking?"

"Yeah," I took a breath, "that was a little shocking."

"I've never told that to anyone. It's a goddamn Monday and I just told a perfect stranger that I cut the lips off my dead grandfather trying to get at his tongue. Fucking hell, I don't even know your name."

"I can't imagine that's going to help anything."

"Still, I'd like to know. Hell, I just told you I mutilated a corpse."

"So you did. Okay, it's Tanya. Your friends know me as Willow, but my real name is Tanya. But that didn't change a thing, now did it?"

"No, it didn't. You're right. Your name doesn't make one lick of difference."

~~~~~~

As Miguel had instructed, I called him after the monkey had been delivered. When he answered, I asked, "Miguel?"

"Is Miguel."

"It's Willow."

There was silence and then a quick burst of Spanish and then, "Don't hang up."

"I don't imagine I'd call just to hang up on you."

"Don't hang up. You, Willow, don't hang up the telephone."

I was laughing through his panic. Then, "Tony has the baby," and laughed again at how code that sounded.

"The baby?"

"The monkey baby."

"Tony has?"

"Yes." And when he didn't speak, I added, "I thought you should know, in case, oh, I don't know, he did something dodgy."

"Dodgy?"

"Crazy or wrong."

"*You* think *he* is crazy?"

"Well, I happen to know he is. But anyway, the Carmen Ghia is at the Merida airport."

"Yes, I know this."

"I messed it up. Sorry about that."

"No problem. How you destroy the car, I don't understand, but it's no problem."

I heard him breathing and didn't imagine there was anything else to say. "Well, I just thought you should know. I'll be going."

"No, don't hang up. The baby is where I tell you to go?"

"Yes."

"Why?" I was hanging up the phone hearing a stream of flummoxed Spanish and the question again, "¿Por qué? Why?"

The Difference Between Neurotics and Psychotics

There was a four thousand dollar refrigerator in the kitchen, sapphires on my fingers, and a Mustang convertible in the backyard. Ed saw none of it.

The front gardens had just been landscaped, the kitchen retiled, and I'd taken a sudden liking to black leather furniture. Ed didn't question it.

He had a new wardrobe, I had a new wardrobe, and the cat had a jeweled collar. But it meant nothing to Ed.

His friends saw it though. They pushed him to ask. "I mean really, man, what is she doing? How does she afford it?"

Ed said, "She is really good with money."

His friends stared at him in wide-eyed disbelief.

He asked me later, "You wouldn't spend three hundred dollars on a pair of jeans, would you?"

"Of course not. That's ridiculous."

Ed went back to his friends and defended me, "No, she's not doing anything."

For nearly two years, he was blind to it all. He'd wake up at 2:00 a.m. to find me gone, and then hear me return with the sun. I'd say, "I was possessed to buy chocolate," or pencils, or bullets, "and ran into a friend." And he'd always believe me.

He had asked only once, "Are you seeing someone?"

And I told the truth, "No, sex is your weakness, not mine." It was all there in my answer, but he had forgotten what my weakness was.

He saw none of the overt evidence, but he spotted the paper-thin edge of a manila envelope wedged between the reference books on the bottom shelf of my bookcase.

He walked with it into the living room where I was reading and asked, "Why do you have all these birth certificates?"

I was staring stupid at the envelope wondering, *How*? How did he see that but not the extravagant wool rug under his feet? I looked into his face. He knew what he'd found, but he wanted to believe that he had caught it early.

He was so utterly clueless.

For two years he hadn't heard a thing I'd said. He'd listened to none of my warnings or the warnings of his friends. He was indifferent to my pleading and patronized my tears. He lived in the woods with no passion for me or our life.

And now he wanted answers, but he didn't know where he was standing. I could see it all clearly though. I knew exactly where this confrontation placed us.

We were on the precipice and freedom was at the bottom of the cliff.

I should have been able to string something together and talk my way clear of it, but he was so earnest and hurt and confounded, and I was genuinely sick of lying to him.

He fanned through the documents asking, "Who are these people?"

There was no explanation he was going to like, so I looked away.

"What have you been doing?"

I shrugged my shoulders.

"How long have you been doing this?"

But I wasn't saying.

He took a week's leave to tear apart the house. He was looking for the little things, the hidden things, but my other secrets were buried.

He called his friends to ask what they knew. They knew very little but they suspected a lot. He spent hours on the phone looking ashen and weak.

When he finally thought he'd pieced it all together and fully understood, he hid the car keys and locked the doors. Then he turned into the dread inquisitor with only one question, "What have you been doing?"

For five days, I didn't get three feet from him, couldn't take a shower, read a book, or walk a straight line through the house without dodging him and the question, "What have you been doing?"

He'd wake me up to ask again and again, "What have you been doing?"

But I wasn't saying.

I was looking over the cliff, wondering what freedom would be like.

There were so many things I wanted to do. I was a con artist with a mind full of schemes. I had been willing to give up my illicit desires while my love for Ed was pleasant, but now that it was painful, it seemed pointless, and it was also just simply in the way. I wanted to be rid of it.

Ed asked, "What have you been doing?"

And I almost said, but the truth was too much. What had I been doing? Oh my god, what had I *not* been doing? I didn't think he could handle it.

He asked again and again. For five days we didn't leave the house. We spoke with no one. He just asked over and over, "What have you been doing?"

It was an interrogation that had turned into torture until finally he offered, "We'll go for a ride," as though it would be a break from the oppression. But once behind the wheel, he had a moment of insanity, driving like when we had first met, racing through the curves at a hundred, demanding, "What have you been doing?"

But I still wasn't saying, so he ripped through the airport gate to bury the speedometer in a race down the runway, shouting, "Is this what you want? You want fear? You want excitement? You want me to scare you?"

Yes, yes, and yes, and it earned him the truth. "I wish you had cared so much a year ago, but it's far too late to court me back now."

AFTERWORD

THE DIFFERENCE BETWEEN NEUROTICS, PSYCHOTICS, AND SOCIOPATHS

I've been told that ending was a bit abrupt and I made myself look like a psychotic bitch. Those in my life now would like me to explain a little further so they don't look like fools for trusting or loving me.

I am easily compelled because I have no desire to be hated. I would prefer to be liked. A true psychopath doesn't care what anyone thinks, and for the most part, neither do I, but given a choice, I would much rather be loved than loathed.

A clinical psychologist once informed me, "You are a little bit of a psychopath," but then corrected himself, "No, that's like being a little bit pregnant. Either you are or you're not."

I am not. I know I am not a psychopath because I have an uncomfortable level of empathy that makes me cry when others shed tears. I wish I didn't. I would probably prefer to be a psychopath because it would involve a lot less headaches. Every time one of you—be you stranger, friend, or family—every time one of you falls apart and I know about it, I cry with you, and your pain gives me a migraine.

I assure you, I am not a psychopath; but I am a sociopath, which is to say I am an anti-social delinquent. Prisons are full of sociopaths and psychopaths, but when questioned, the imprisoned sociopath will honestly admit that they will commit any number of crimes to help a friend.

A friend will help you move; a true friend will help you move a body.

A friend will bail you out of jail; a true friend will be sitting beside you.

Who wouldn't want to have a true friend? But they sound a lot like a sociopath.

A psychopath will betray you when you are no longer of use; a sociopath will go to jail for you. That's not an absolute truth but is broadly accurate.

I would go to jail for a friend, but I have also come pretty close to putting my friends in jail. I am the best friend to have at the worst of times, and the most unsettling friend to have the rest of the time.

So there we have the difference between psychopaths and sociopaths. Next we have the neurotics. Now that's a hard one for me to understand, but it includes all you obsessive-compulsives, the excessively guilty, and the unaccountably anxious. I am so far from neurotic, I don't dare try to explain it further, but I know Ed was neurotic.

He had a number of obsessions but his biggest compulsion was to speak the truth. He could not even lie to a telemarketer, would not tell them I was not at home, or in the shower, or otherwise occupied when I was not. That was lying, and Ed did not lie.

He wanted open honesty in all relationships, and that included the fleeting one he had on the phone with sales people. They'd call up all chipper and unsuspecting to sell a product, completely clueless the person on the other end was about to dismantle their lives. The honest exchange of information could take a while, but by the end of the hour, Ed would have the poor soul sobbing on line, crying over the deceit in his life, confessing his every sin, and admitting he was only in sales because he'd been molested by his uncle as a child.

Sometimes I'd take pity and pull the phone away early to caution, "You have made a big mistake calling this house, and if you call back, I am not going to save you twice. Call again and you'll end up in fetal position on the carpeted floor of your cubicle, begging for your mommy, and when you end up on mental disability, you'll wish you had listened to me."

Ed was on a crusade to turn the world honest. His path to enlightenment was brightly lit by the truth and few people could hide deep enough in the shadows not to be illuminated.

It didn't make him happy though. He wasn't happy. He was honest.

From what I'd witnessed, honesty didn't really make anyone happy. The truth was a punch to the gut, and while you were falling, a knee to the face, then you could lie on the floor and bleed for a spell.

Ed put me on the floor a few times and did more damage to me than Sergiu ever could.

After six years together, Ed knew how to knock me down and tear me apart, and I knew how to adjust the mirrors so he was blinded by all that bright white truth.

As with any divorce, there was much more to our breakup than could be explained in a sentence, but we still tried. We told everyone the fault was mine, that Ed wanted children but I wouldn't agree. It made things simple.

But between the two of us, we thought the fault started with the other. I thought I had merely overreacted to what Ed was doing, and Ed didn't think he had done anything wrong. To those closest to Ed and I, who knew the full details of our divorce, they thought we had both acted in appalling ways.

But still Ed said to me, "If we were to tell any normal person out there," in acceptable society he meant, "what each of us had done, they would all think what you did was worse."

I've told the largest part of what I did, but there was more happening than just my crimes. I will never divulge Ed's part, so I can't know if he was right. Maybe he was, and I alone would get the blame, but I suspect most of you so-called normal people would step back and say, "You both deserved what you got."

My offenses were felonious and could have put me in jail, and in Ed's defense, he never once lied to me. He was at all times brutally honest. In return, I gave him what I would have preferred, the comfort of a lie, the courtesy of concealment.

Years later, a cruel lover would ask, "Are you lying to me?"

And I answered with blunt honesty, "I don't care enough about you to lie."

In the end, that was the essence of my love for Ed. I loved him enough to lie when I thought we could fix it, and I respected his desire for the truth when I knew it was past repair.

Ed was neurotically honest and he taught me to be psychotically honest.

I suspect Ed would deny it, but I understand why he was so fully committed to speaking the truth. The absolute truth is a wicked sort of rush. It's far more amusing than any lie. Both have the potential to empower and to hurt, but the truth is emotionally superior. Few people could fault you for it, not when you've got ethics on your side. The truth is morally unassailable.

But it has no pity. It is merciless.

And the truth is, if I don't love you, I am one of the most honest people you are ever likely to meet. Well, that and you have to know my real name.

CONTACT

The second book in the *Criminal Mischief* series is called *The Expatriates*. You'll find the first chapter below.

For more about this series, or to contact me, please visit tanyathompsonbooks.com

My website is also where you can find copies of the newspaper and magazine articles mentioned in the book.

THE EXPATRIATES

Possession really isn't nine-tenths of the law. If it were, I wouldn't have been worried.

I was on the side of the road in Texas with eight squad cars. They'd surrounded both me and the 5-speed convertible that was in my possession. I'd just crossed one county line into another, so I had city police, state troopers, and two sheriff's departments to contend with.

And the little red Mustang was stolen.

I'd driven it off a dealer's lot for a test drive that was going on close to a year, and things had been going so well, I couldn't think of a reason to take it back.

The paper dealer tags had blown off shortly after it topped a hundred, so, to avoid any hassle with the cops, I'd taken the tags and registration from my 1979 Mustang and applied them to the 1990 model. And then, just to keep things tidy, I got a little help moving the VIN plate over as well.

I'd already been pulled over a dozen times with this ridiculous set-up, but that had always been in Tennessee where I could play *I know your mamma.*

It's a great game. "I know your mamma" is how it starts.

"You know my mamma?"

"I sure do. She invited me to church." If you're in the South, you can safely rely on the officer's family attending Sunday service. You can also assume they meet afterwards for lunch—which is called dinner—and at least one relative has had a recent misfortune. "Your mamma wanted me to come round for dinner, but I had to go up to the hospital to see that cousin of ours."

"You related to Bubba?"

"You didn't know we were related? That's how I know your mamma."

"Well, I'll be."

And that's generally the end of it.

But in Texas, I had Tennessee plates and no one was going to believe I knew their mamma.

Twenty miles before, I'd lit up a deputy's speed gun with a triple digit number that left him ten minutes behind. He'd radioed for help, and I was the only thing happening in Texas that hour.

By the time one squad car caught up, seven more were descending.

The sheriff, police, and state troopers from one county were driving straight into a similar group that was cutting across the interstate median from the next, and I was wondering who did what to whom for all the attention.

The entire south bound lane of traffic came to a stop and I was surprised to be singled out.

Once we all got onto the side of the road, twelve men in seven different uniforms held a conference to discuss who got to claim responsibility for the drug bust.

I asked, "Drug bust? What drug bust?"

And one of them said, "We know you're smuggling."

"Smuggling?" *Dear god*, "Smuggling what?"

"Drugs, obviously."

"How is that obvious?"

"You're a lone woman traveling through Texas from out-of-state."

"Oh. It's obvious then." But it wasn't. I wasn't smuggling drugs. I was driving to Central America with a stolen car for no other reason than it amused me.

And it was still pretty amusing until one officer started checking my registration against the VIN. Nobody had ever done that before. I had never let it get that far.

The VIN plate had been attached with Crazy Glue, and I had no idea how it was fairing with the temperature over a hundred. I needed to get the situation under control, but Tennessee games weren't going to play in Texas. I'd have to know someone higher than their mammas. I was running the possibilities through my mind, "I know your mayor. Your governor? *Your God*?"

Then another officer was calling in my license while five more invited me out of the car to debate which could detain me, and the remaining six didn't wait for my consent to search.

I was pretty certain there was not enough charm in the world to bring them all back into conference again.

And the numbers were against me. Of the twelve officers assembled, one of them surely knew the difference between a 79 Mustang and a model that was only three years old. Surely.

Switching the VIN and tags no longer seemed such a clever trick. I wondered why I thought I could get away with it.

I watched one officer stop the cd player and another lower the power windows.

Power-freaking-windows. Blessed hell.

I tried to think of who to call for bail.

After fifteen minutes of removing the door panels, the spare tire and the backseat, one of the officers finally turned his attention to my overnight case. It was a vintage piece from the 1930s and he didn't know which end was up. He put his fingers on the double locks to flip them back, and I said aloud, "Oh, dear god, no."

It snapped every officer's attention onto the piece, onto me, then back to the luggage.

They knew they had finally found the stash. They were elated. From one county, a deputy took hold of my arm to claim me as their own, and from the other county, a second deputy pulled me back.

Then the luggage spewed makeup, perfume, and tampons across the asphalt.

I shook my head and explained, "He opened it upside down."

They were mortified. There wasn't a man among them that knew what to do with the articles littering the road, and to ensure none of them had to contemplate it, the search was called off.

"I was sure we had a case," said one of the sheriffs.

"I have never been so certain," confirmed a Trooper.

"*Really?*" I asked. "Do I look like a drug smuggler?"

"Yes, ma'am, you do."

"I do?"

"Single woman traveling alone," the sheriff explained, and all the officers shook their heads to agree that it would look as such.

"I hate that I look like a drug smuggler," I frowned. "I'd rather look like something more appealing, like, oh, I don't know..." I couldn't believe I was actually going to say it, but I did, "... like a car thief.

"Well, we get quite a few of those down here too."

"*Really*? How very exciting. So what does a car thief look like?"

They all stared at me like they had only just realized I was an idiot, and I had to tell myself to shut up before they figured out what kind.

~~~~~~

I often had to tell myself to shut up. After three weeks driving south through Mexico, I was at the Belize border trying to convince the custom's official that the value of the Mustang was $500. If I wanted to enter the country with it, I'd have to pay 100% tax.

I said, "Ok, here's five hundred US cash."

He looked at the cash and then at the car. It looked like we might have a deal, but then he reconsidered. Running his hand over the plush upholstery, his accent seemed to become heavier, more Caribbean, "This car be worth more than five-hundred on the island."

He was undoubtedly correct, but I had to know, "What island?"

"This island."

"What island?"

"This be Belize island."

Belize was settled by freed and emancipated slaves, so the majority of the population spoke English Creole. I thought we might be having a language problem, so I asked again, *Where* is this island?"

He pointed under his feet, "This be Belize island."

"Belize is an island?"

"Yes!"

I didn't know what to do with that. I'd taken off from Tennessee without a map, so I had nothing to prove it wasn't.

But it wasn't.

I had to know, "Where are you from?"

"I be from the island."

"This island?"

"Ya, this island we be standing on."

I couldn't decide if he was stupid or if he was toying with me. I stared at him crooked for several moments hoping the truth would reveal itself and when it didn't, I held up my hands to concede, "Ok, an island it is. I'd like to enter the island."

"Tax on car be fifty thousand dollars."

"It's not an island."

"Belize be island. Tax be fifty thousand."

"You want that in cash?" I was a little sarcastic.

But he was sincere, "Or credit card."

I might have gone with credit if I'd been traveling with cards that weren't in my name, but I'd left all my erroneous identities in the

States. The only illicit thing in my possession was the car. And the custom's official was starting to look at the paperwork with suspicion.

I decided it was time to leave. "I'm just going to pop back across the border to Mexico."

He squinted harder at the forms, curious to read, "One nine, seven nine."

"One of the banks over there might help me secure that fifty-thousand."

"Nineteen seven nine."

"Why don't you just hold this five-hundred as a deposit?"

"Nineteen seventy nine?"

"I don't need a receipt."

"This year be wrong." He began to circle the car with the form and my registration.

"Was that a picture of your mamma I saw inside?"

He looked up from the rounded headlights. "Where is this picture?"

"Inside. There was a picture of a lovely woman on the desk."

"*Ah, ha, ha,*" he laughed. "You see my beautiful woman?"

"I assumed it was your mother, considering ..." I looked him up and down. "She's lovely."

"My madda is very pretty. You can see this?"

"Oh, absolutely. I'd never doubt it. I imagine all your brothers and sisters look like her too. How many siblings have you got?"

"We be big family. My madda raise eight children with no man."

"Bless her heart, she's a saint."

"My madda *is* a saint. But you," he exhaled slow and seemed sad to look at the Mustang. "What I do with you?"

"Oh, don't worry about me. I'm no hassle. Keep the five-hundred as a deposit and I'll be back tomorrow with more."

He smiled.

I smiled.

Things were looking good.

"I like this car," he said.

I raised my eyes to agree it was a likeable car.

"Do you think I would look good in this car?"

My smile was hopeful that this was not about to happen.

But he continued, "I could get many a woman in this car."

I frowned. "It's not really a man's car. It's pretty girly. I could see you in a Camaro, or a Cadillac. Yes, a Cadillac would suit you better."

"But there is no Cadillac here."

Hmm. No, there wasn't.

"I show you a story." He motioned me to follow him back into the Immigration building. "Can you read?" he handed me a newspaper.

"Yes."

"Then read," he pointed at the front page headline.

And I questioned, "'No Second Chance'?"

"Read it."

The story was about a father and son who had broken into a private home to steal an old television and what must have been one hell of a paper towel holder. It was their first and last offense because the judge sentenced them to life in jail.

"We take theft very serious on the island."

"I see that."

"A stolen car would be very serious."

"I imagine so."

He asked again, "Do you think I would look good in that car?"

And I was certain, "Yes. Yes, I think you would look better in that car than me."

~~~~~~~

When I first heard about Belize, it had been described as full of liars, criminals, and exiles.

"Liars, criminals, and exiles?" I might as well have been told they were handing out royal titles and I could be the queen. "The place sounds divine. I have to see it."

My friends took this announcement with all due horror. They tried to persuade, threaten, and warn against it.

"How safe is Belize for a single woman?" one friend asked a retired Army officer who knew me just well enough.

He said, "For any cautious woman, with a sense of restraint and self-preservation, it is safe enough. But for Tanya? Tanya will be dead in three months."

I remember my triumphant return. "Ha," I boasted, "I was there for three months and I lived."

To which the wise Army officer replied, "Yes, but had you remained a day longer, would you be?"

He had a point.

But I thought my sense of self-preservation was a little better than he imagined. After all, I'd made it through customs with my freedom. And it seemed I now had a friend at the border. We shared a secret that could put us both in jail, but neither of us seemed the sort to talk.

The custom's official gave me a ride to the bus, and I had to admit, "The car does suit you."

"Any time you want, girl, I be here for you. I drive you anywhere you want. Or you could stay. I take you home to my madda."

I didn't think I'd ever see him again, but it seemed polite to suggest, "We'll have dinner on my way back north."

I wasn't in the least upset about the way things had turned out—the Mustang wasn't mine to be upset about—but it was strange being without a car.

And public transport was unlike anything I had experienced. From the outside, it was just an old school bus still painted yellow from the States, but inside, tasseled upholstery fringe was strung across the windows with multi-colored Christmas lights, and South African reggae played from speakers bolted to the roof. The bus stopped at a field between the border and the capital so that forty men with machetes could board. One of them fell asleep on my shoulder, and nothing I was prepared to do would wake him up.

After six weeks of touring the country, I understood I had to share a seat already occupied by a woman if I didn't want a man nuzzling into my neck, but little else had occurred to make me think I wouldn't live another six weeks. I was fairly certain the three month prediction of my demise was inaccurate.

Belize wasn't exciting enough to be deadly. It was certainly full of liars, criminals, and exiles, but they all seemed to be retired.

And when I stopped long enough to think about it, I was pretty tired too. I'd divorced shortly before leaving Tennessee, and even though it had been a friendly parting, divorce is something that starts a long time before the paperwork is finalized and finishes a long time after.

Divorce is exhausting.

So is non-stop traveling.

When I arrived in San Ignacio on Belize's western border, I was so drained of energy, so desperate for a touch of stability, I decided to stay. I thought I might stay forever. But that was before meeting the crazy American.

~~~~~~

IF YOU'RE NOT COMPLETELY SICK OF MY PERSONALITY BY NOW, YOU'LL FIND MORE INFORMATION ON **THE EXPATRIATES** *AT MY WEBSITE TANYATHOMPSONBOOKS.COM*